TREASURES
OF ANCIENT
NIGERIA

TREASURES OF ANCIENT NIGERIA

TEXT BY EKPO EYO
AND FRANK WILLETT

ALFRED A. KNOPF   NEW YORK
in association with The Detroit Institute of Arts, 1980

THIS IS A BORZOI BOOK PUBLISHED BY ALFRED A. KNOPF, INC.

LC 79-3497
ISBN 0-394-50975-7 (Knopf)
ISBN 0-394-73858-6 (pbk.)

Manufactured in the United States of America

First Edition

EDITOR: ROLLYN O. KRICHBAUM
PHOTOGRAPHER: DIRK BAKKER
DESIGNER: BETTY BINNS

Photographs not taken by Dirk Bakker were provided by the following people and institutions:
Frank Willett, figs. 1, 2, 6, 13, 14, 17, 18, 20−37, nos. 66, 93; Thurston Shaw, figs. 4, 5, 19;
Ekpo Eyo, figs. 3, 7−9, 11; British Museum, figs. 10, 12; Phillips Stevens, Jr., fig. 15; Philip
Allison, fig. 16.

FRONT COVER: *number 42*
BACK COVER: *numbers 81 and 82*
FRONTISPIECE: *number 16*

This book is published in conjunction with a major loan exhibition of works from the Nigerian National Museums, organized by The Detroit Institute of Arts and made possible through grants from the National Endowment for the Arts, a Federal Agency; the National Foundation on the Arts and Humanities, Arts and Artifacts Indemnity Act; the Michigan Council for the Arts; and Mobil Companies Nigeria.

DIRECTOR OF THE EXHIBITION: MICHAEL KAN, *Deputy Director and Curator of African, Oceanic, and New World Cultures at The Detroit Institute of Arts*.

GUEST CURATOR: DR. EKPO EYO, *Director, Nigerian National Museums, and Director, Federal Department of Antiquities, Lagos*.

The exhibition has the following traveling itinerary:

THE DETROIT INSTITUTE OF ARTS: January 17 through March 16, 1980

THE CALIFORNIA PALACE OF THE LEGION OF HONOR, SAN FRANCISCO: April 28 through June 29, 1980

THE METROPOLITAN MUSEUM OF ART, NEW YORK: August 11 through October 12, 1980

CONTENTS

FOREWORD

TREASURES OF ANCIENT NIGERIA is a historic exhibition of international importance. It is the first time that the Nigerian government has extended a major loan of its art treasures, many of which have only been recovered during the last forty years. Westerners have long associated African art with wooden sculpture, which does not survive, in most African climates, for more than about one hundred years; hence, collectors and even scholars are largely attuned to recent traditions rather than to those that are more ancient. "Treasures of Ancient Nigeria" should correct this misconception. These one hundred works of art, spanning some two thousand years, are made of such durable materials as terracotta, bronze, and ivory, and are of such high quality that they rank with the greatest art created by mankind.

The exhibition, initiated by Michael Kan, Deputy Director of The Detroit Institute of Arts and Curator of African, Oceanic, and New World Cultures, was made possible through the complete cooperation of Dr. Ekpo Eyo, head of the National Museums of Nigeria and Guest Curator of this exhibition. We are also grateful to Congressman Charles Diggs, Jr.; Andrew Young, former United States Ambassador to the United Nations; Donald Easum, former United States Ambassador to Nigeria and now President of the African American Institute, New York City; Olujimi Jolaoso, Nigerian Ambassador to the United States; Arthur Lewis, former Public Affairs Officer, United States Inter-national Communication Agency (U.S.I.C.A.), and now Assistant Director, African Affairs, U.S.I.C.A., Washington, D.C.; Samuel Thomsen and Robert Plotkin, Cultural Affairs officers, American Embassy, Lagos; and Ade James, Senior Cultural Specialist, U.S.I.C.A., American Embassy, Lagos. We are indebted to the African American Institute, which originally was to receive the exhibition and which was responsible for its New York appearance. Many other people have contributed to the exhibition and catalogue and they are appropriately acknowledged in Michael Kan's Preface.

Important financial aid has been received from the National Endowment for the Arts, the Michigan Council for the Arts, and Mobil Companies Nigeria. Overseas loan insurance has been largely defrayed by the National Foundation on the Arts and Humanities, Arts and Artifacts Indemnity Act. The American Association of Dealers in Ancient, Oriental, and Primitive Art provided appraisals of the objects for insurance purposes. Without all this assistance, both the exhibition and the book that accompanies it would have been impossible.

FREDERICK J. CUMMINGS
Director, The Detroit Institute of Arts
IAN McKIBBON WHITE
Director, The Fine Arts Museums of San Francisco
PHILIPPE de MONTEBELLO
Director, The Metropolitan Museum of Art

PREFACE

It is ironic that the most important African art pre-dating 1900 is the least known African art in the Western world. Of all these works, and some of them date back two thousand years, nine-tenths are Nigerian. Most of them, however, have remained buried in the ground until quite recently. Only in the case of the Benin bronzes have they been widely known and distributed throughout the world.

As a result of the British Punitive Expedition of 1897, more than two thousand Benin pieces were shipped to Britain. Their importance was immediately recognized by the early German Africanist Felix von Luschan. Writing in 1919, he described them in these glowing terms: "Benvenuto Cellini could not have cast them better, and nobody else either, before or since Cellini....These bronzes are technically of the highest quality possible."

The presence of Benin works in Europe helped create a growing respect for African art and, less than ten years later, artists such as Pablo Picasso and Georges Braque were using African art as models in their rejection of imitative in favor of conceptual art. The works these artists turned to, however, were not Nigerian, but were from the French, Belgian, and German colonies. The official policy in these colonies was to discourage and suppress the traditional ways of life and replace them with Christian education and civilization. The British, on the other hand, favored a more indirect kind of rule, leaving Nigeria's traditional culture alone to a greater extent. Since the arts were an integral part of the living culture, when European demand created a commercial market,

it was the French, German, and Belgian territories that lost much of their heritage, while Nigeria's remained largely intact.

It would be a mistake, however, to leave the impression that the British colonial government fostered the protection of Nigeria's cultural heritage. In fact, it took a completely uninterested position. But, fortunately, there was one Englishman, named Kenneth Murray, who was devoted to the Nigerian people and their traditional culture. For many years he labored to preserve Nigeria's art and, perhaps more important, worked with Nigerians who wanted to preserve and transmit their ancient heritage.

Murray first came to Nigeria from England in the service of the colonial government in 1927 and was assigned to teach art in government schools. He spent a great deal of time studying pottery and its techniques throughout Nigeria and became convinced that there was an urgent need to collect traditional art objects and record the context of their manufacture and use before these traditions disappeared under the impact of European culture.

It was during this period that the Igbo-Ukwu and the Ife bronzes first came to light, and Murray's involvement with these finds is well recounted in Dr. Eyo's Introduction. Suffice it to say here that when Murray heard about the discoveries, he immediately realized their importance and tried to see that the works were protected.

It was also at this time that William Fagg was named Assistant Keeper of Ethnography at the

British Museum. Although Fagg never held an official position in Nigeria, throughout the years that followed he was more responsible than anyone else for bringing Nigerian art before the international art community. His 1960 exhibition of Nigerian masterpieces in honor of Nigerian independence constituted a veritable landmark. While at the British Museum, he became intimately familiar with the Benin works, so many of which were in the museum, and through his brother, Bernard, a young administrative officer with archaeological interests who worked in Nigeria from 1939 until 1963, he knew about the discoveries of other objects as they were found.

In 1943, the colonial government was finally persuaded to set up the Antiquities Service (later the Department of Antiquities) with Kenneth Murray as its head. The new department started immediately to make a conscious effort to prevent the unauthorized export of traditional Nigerian art. It was also in 1943 that Bernard Fagg, who happened to be stationed in the Plateau region, first identified the Nok culture. Tin miners uncovered a terracotta head that was eventually shown to Fagg, who recognized that this work was from an unknown culture. The first museums established by the Department of Antiquities were at places like Esie and Oron, where there were specific groups of objects that had been brought together for one reason or another. In 1946, the Benin Museum was founded to house works that were found in situ or that were returned to their original homeland. The first proper museum with display and study areas was the Ife Museum, which was finished in 1948. Unfortunately, serious defects developed in the roof so it was not opened until early in 1954.

During the 1950s, Murray started to develop a concept for a national museum system. It was his view that Nigeria, being so vast, needed a whole series of museums, each of which could concentrate on the culture of the immediate area but would also show the other cultures of the country as well. With independence anticipated at this time, it was planned that every state capital would have its own museum. The government was very interested in bringing Nigeria's diverse population together, and the museums became an important instrument of this policy. Jos, which opened in 1952, was the first national, as opposed to regional, museum and showed material and art from all over Nigeria. It was during this time that several Nigerians came into the department to train in museum work.

In 1957, Bernard Fagg was named Director of the Department of Antiquities and in the same year the Lagos Museum was founded. The museum was designed to emphasize broad cultural similarities, cutting across many linguistic boundaries. Its mission was to foster understanding among the peoples of Nigeria. In this scheme of things, the education department became increasingly important, and its exhibits didactic rather than art historical.

Throughout all these years, Nigerian art had been studied from an archaeologist's and anthropologist's point of view, rather than from an art historian's perspective. In 1956, a young Oxford-trained archaeologist named Frank Willett went out to Nigeria to excavate at Ife, and succeeded in bridging this gap. Willett came under Murray's influence and stayed on as Curator at the Ife Museum, where he carefully catalogued its collection and instituted a program of professional museum practices. After leaving Nigeria in 1963, he took a post at Northwestern University, Evanston, Illinois, in its art history department, lifting African art out of ethnography and properly placing it in the discipline of art history. He also published, in 1967, an important book on Ife art in its historical context. Willett's continuing research and publications, including over seventy-five articles, have helped keep Nigerian art before the scholarly public. He also published a book for the layman in 1971, *African Art,* probably the best introduction there is on the subject.

I come now to Dr. Ekpo Eyo, the present Director of the Federal Department of Antiquities and head of the whole Nigerian museum system. Dr. Eyo, trained at Cambridge and the University of Ibadan, is an archaeologist and a man with vast knowledge of Nigeria's people and cultures who has himself conducted important excavations at Ife and Owo. His Owo finds, in fact, provide the first concrete evidence of a cultural link between Ife and Benin art. But his contributions, like Willett's, go far beyond his excavations. Since he became Assistant Director of Antiquities in 1965 and Director in 1968, he has embarked on an ambitious plan, which includes a new building for the Lagos Museum, soon to open, with special wings for natural history, modern art, and education facilities. He has encouraged archaeological and ethnographic research and has initiated a program to publish monographs covering all phases of Nigerian culture. He has started to build four new museums, at Maiduguri (Borno State), Sokota (Sokoto State), Ibadan (Oyo State), and Enugu (Anambra State). Finally, at Jos, he has set aside sixty-five acres of land where reproductions of classic buildings from all over Nigeria will be built.

Dr. Eyo's work has not been confined to Nigeria. He has traveled literally all over the world in Nigeria's behalf. Active in UNESCO's International Council of Museums and the Commonwealth Association of Museums, he has spoken eloquently on Africa's right to some of the art that was taken out during the colonial period. Dr. Eyo's participation with The Detroit Institute of Arts is another aspect of his work with the international museum community. In agreeing to this loan — in effect, the best of his country's ancient artistic legacy — he has exhibited a generosity and cooperation that is indeed extraordinary.

Many people have worked hard to make this exhibition and catalogue a reality. My deepest appreciation goes to Dr. Eyo, who, as Guest Curator, selected the objects and co-authored the catalogue, and, in addition, smoothed the way for many trips various people had to make to Nigeria. Frank Willett, now Director of the Hunterian Museum, Glasgow, co-authored the catalogue and served as advisor on many aspects of the exhibition, particularly its educational components. His contributions have been invaluable. Several other people are to be thanked for their work on the catalogue, in particular, Rollyn O. Krichbaum, editor, Dirk Bakker, photographer, and Betty Binns, designer.

The staff of the National Museum, Lagos, is to be thanked for their cooperation, particularly Emmanuel Arinze, Patrick Okpalla, and Daniel Kekeke. Many departments of The Detroit Institute of Arts have been involved in planning for this exhibition. I would especially like to thank Bob Weston, Boris Sellers, Abraham Joel, Charles A. Lewis, William Wierzbowski, and Patricia Ryan for their efforts.

I wish to thank Charles Froom for his work on the exhibition's installation. I am grateful to several colleagues in the field for their interest and advice, particularly Dr. Roy Sieber, Dr. Douglas Fraser, Douglas Newton, and Susan Vogel. Finally, I wish to thank Dr. Frederick J. Cummings, Director of The Detroit Institute of Arts, for his constant encouragement and support.

MICHAEL KAN
Deputy Director and Curator of African,
Oceanic, and New World Cultures,
The Detroit Institute of Arts

TREASURES
OF ANCIENT
NIGERIA

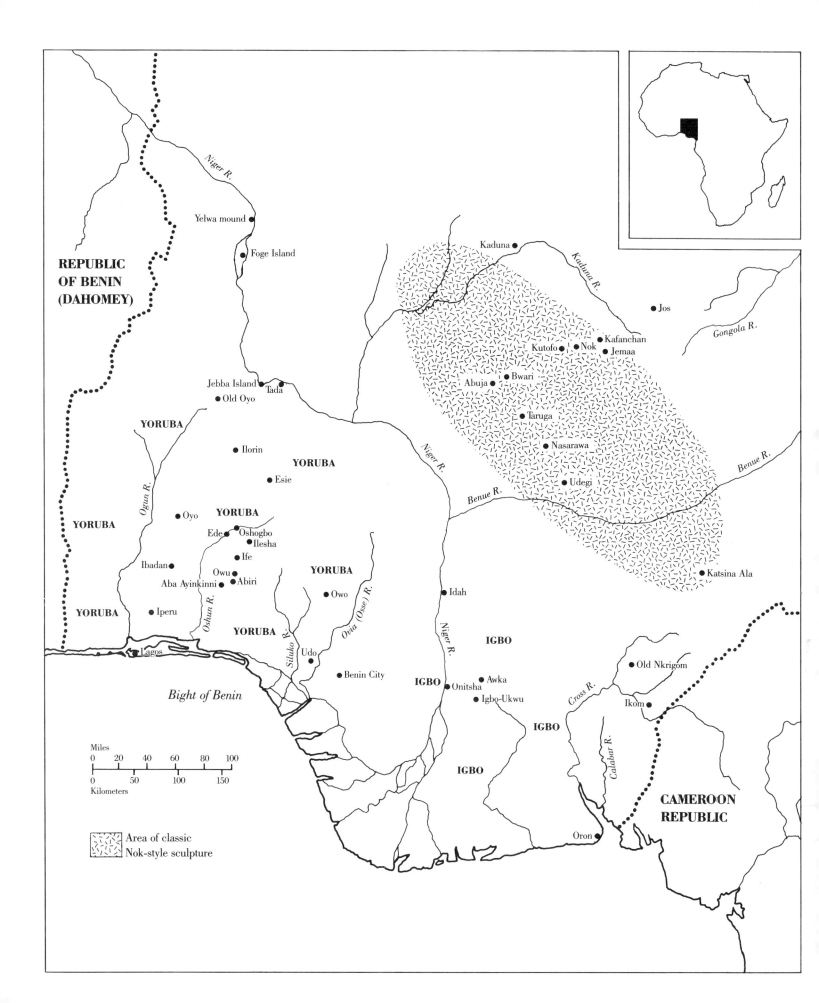

REPUBLIC
OF BENIN
(DAHOMEY)

Niger R.

Yelwa mound

Foge Island

Kaduna

Kaduna R.

Jos

Gongola R.

Kafanchan
Kutofo   Nok   Jemaa

Jebba Island   Tada
Old Oyo

YORUBA

Abuja   Bwari

Ilorin

YORUBA

Taruga

Esie

Niger R.

Nasarawa

YORUBA

Oyo

Ogun R.

YORUBA

Ede   Oshogbo
Ilesha
Ife

Udegi

Benue R.

Benue R.

Ibadan

Owu

Aba Ayinkinni   Abiri

YORUBA

Owo

Ovia (Osse) R.

Katsina Ala

Iperu

Oshun R.

YORUBA

Idah

Siluko R.

Udo

Niger R.

IGBO

Old Nkrigom

Lagos

Benin City

IGBO

Onitsha   Awka

Igbo-Ukwu

Cross R.

Ikom

Bight of Benin

IGBO

IGBO

Calabar R.

**CAMEROON
REPUBLIC**

Miles
0   20   40   60   80   100

0   50   100   150
Kilometers

Oron

Area of classic
Nok-style sculpture

INTRODUCTION
EKPO EYO

The government of Nigeria is pleased to lend its art treasures for exhibition in three major American museums. These hundred works, from cultures spanning over two thousand years, belong to Nigeria in particular, but they also belong to mankind at large. Significantly, most of them have never been shown outside Nigeria before. It is our hope that this exhibition will be seen by many Americans, and that this will lead to a better knowledge of the past and present of Nigeria and create a better understanding between our two countries.

In the following pages, I will briefly introduce each culture and tell the story of how each group of works came to be known. In the essay that follows, Professor Frank Willett has taken a look at these works from an art historian's point of view. If the reader notes that at times Professor Willett and I are at variance in what we say, that should not be surprising, for our field is still very young and there are many gray areas that only more work can throw light upon. The data presented here are limited, too, and subject to various interpretations.

Most of the pieces in this exhibition have been uncovered by archaeologists within the last forty years. When one considers the quantity and quality of the pieces that have been found in a limited number of excavations, one cannot help imagining what still remains hidden. It is, therefore, our hope that this exhibition and catalogue will serve to stimulate others to join us in the continuing search for Nigeria's treasures and for the stories behind them.

THE NOK CULTURE

The Nok culture, dated conservatively to between 500 B.C. and A.D. 200, produced the earliest known terracotta sculptures in Africa south of the Sahara. It is actually only since 1943 that there has been a "Nok culture" to speak about. It was in that year that Bernard Fagg, a cadet administrative officer with archaeological training and interests, was shown a head which he realized was of great archaeological importance (no.6). The head had been found by a clerk at a tin mine, who had taken it back to his house and later used it as a scarecrow

3

in his yam fields. It remained there for a year, until the manager of the mine, F. H. Townend, noticed and acquired it and took it to Jos, where Fagg saw it. Fagg realized that this head was similar in style to a monkey head that had been found forty miles away in 1928 by the co-owner of a tin-mining partnership operating around Nok, Colonel J. Dent Young. Young had taken his piece to the mining museum that had been established at Jos, and there it had remained. Almost immediately after he saw the second work, Fagg made it known to all the miners working around the Jos Plateau that the pieces were of historical importance and any more finds should be reported to him. Because the first piece had been found near the small village of Nok —a place you would not find on an ordinary map of Nigeria—and because it is archaeological practice to name a culture after the first place where evi-

dence of it has been found, Fagg named the culture that had produced the pieces of terracotta sculpture the Nok culture.

Since 1943, over one hundred fifty Nok works have been recovered. Most have been stray finds by tin miners working in the Nok Valley west of the Jos Plateau (see map), which is surrounded by rocks out of which tin has been eroded and concentrated by water action into alluvial deposits (figs. 1 and 2). Some works have also been found during excavations conducted by Bernard and Angela Fagg and Robert Soper. Although much remains unknown, we have now begun to piece together information about this culture.

First of all, the culture and the art associated with it (nos. 1–14) do not appear to represent the begin-

Figure 1 Tin miners in the Big Paddok at Nok dig down through several levels of alluvial deposits to reach the tin. It is within these deposits that most Nok works have been found.

ning of a tradition. The art is too complex and sophisticated to have been made in the earliest stages of an evolving culture. We see this art after it has developed over quite a long period of time, but where it began, we do not know. One day, perhaps, a more ancient culture that gave birth to Nok will be discovered.

Nok pieces show a series of common characteristics — most notably the treatment of the eyes and the piercing of the eyes, nostrils, and ears — and have been found over a very large area. These common traits, along with the geographical distribution over an area of three hundred miles by a hundred miles north of where the River Benue meets the River Niger, make us hypothesize that these people lived in a hierarchically structured society, with a common focus of either political or religious power. Although we can infer little about the actual political institutions of the people because there are no oral traditions that relate to them, Bernard Fagg has suggested that they were the speakers of proto-Bantu (as defined by Joseph Greenberg) who later spread across the whole of central and southern Africa. At the present time, this area in central Nigeria is occupied by a variety of different groups, some quite small and some quite large.

With regard to their religion, we can only make certain inferences. Several animals are represented in this sculpture: for example, an elephant (no. 13), snakes, monkeys, a tick, and so on. Were these representations merely a record of the world around them or were they an integral part of the system of belief? Elsewhere in this catalogue, Pro-

Figure 2 Another view of tin miners in the Nok Valley.

Figure 3 *This fragment of a Nok terracotta shows a hoe or axe on the shoulder of a farmer.*

fessor Willett has cautiously suggested that it was the belief in witchcraft that might have been responsible for the decision not to represent human beings as naturalistically as animals. That might well be, but the detailed representation of animals might also suggest that animals played an important role in these people's religious beliefs, as is the case in so many cultures throughout the world.

The natural environment that produced this culture is nowadays mostly savannah. It probably was the same kind of environment in the past, although there is evidence that the present forest region to the south reached further north than where it is today. The vegetable remains recovered from the waterlogged deposits suggest that the area may have been more forested than it is today; but the fact that the Nok remains are found in alluvial deposits in dried-up riverbeds also suggests that these remains were from trees that grew along the riverside where the people lived.

We know the people were agriculturists. A number of grinding stones, otherwise known as querns, which were used in grinding grain, have been found in Nok deposits. There are also two terracotta fragments, each of which depicts a hoe or an axe placed over the shoulder of what we might term a farmer (fig. 3). Some seeds that are oil-bearing and known locally as *atili* have been found in Nok deposits, and it is possible that the Nok people cultivated the plants that had these seeds and then extracted oil from them. We also know that the people who made these works were the earliest known smelters of iron south of the Sahara. Slag from their furnaces and the *tuyères* (clay nozzles for the bellows) they used have been found, which demonstrate that they were very advanced in this technology.

The Nok pieces are highly sophisticated. Particular individuals and animals have been singled out and given special treatment in a very complex way. The artists knew how to select the right kind of clay, mix it with the right kind of other materials, and perfectly fire the objects with a consistency that made it possible for them to survive for more than two thousand years. Furthermore, they were able to translate both their ideas and the images they saw in nature into concrete forms of great power and beauty.

The people who made the Nok pieces loved ornamentation. In the three complete figures (nos. 9, 10, and 12), you can see how profusely they used beads, just like the Ife people after them (fig. 21). If you look at the foot (no. 11), you will see that it is bedecked with rings of either fiber decoration or chain, possibly made of iron. They paid a great deal of attention to their hairdos; the ridged hairstyle of number 6, the buns on number 1, and the knobs on number 7 are good examples. They also used a lot of beads to decorate themselves. Hundreds of quartz beads have been found along with the apparatus for making them. The beads were ground into cylinders in grooves cut in stone, and the holes were made with iron tools, a very ingenious way of manufacturing stone beads.

The Nok works in this exhibition are dated from 500 B.C. We should not look on this as a rigid limit, however, because at least two dates have shown that Nok may have started as early as 900 B.C. The argument against accepting the earlier date is that the two early dates were obtained from below the terracotta sculptures. But the sculptures are so advanced in style that they must have had time to evolve. I think the question must be left open so that people will know there is a possibility Nok might be much older than is generally accepted today.

Professor Willett discusses at some length the relationship between the art of Nok and that of Ife, which we will turn to later. He holds that Ife art was derived either from Nok art, from a related culture, or from another common ancestor. He argues that both art forms executed almost lifesize works in terracotta, with the addition of bronzes in Ife art. He also points out stylistic similarities between both art forms. It is true that some pieces of Nok art are, like Ife art, somewhat naturalistic; nevertheless, most of the objects, and there are many of them, are very stylized. The difficulty of accepting the derivation of Ife art directly from Nok art is that they are separated so widely in terms of space and time. It seems to me that there must be a missing link between the two cultures that we as yet don't know about.

IGBO-UKWU

The discovery of the art of Igbo-Ukwu (nos. 15–38), like most major archaeological discoveries in the world, was accidental. In 1938, a man named Isaiah Anozie in the village of Igbo-Ukwu, a small town near Awka in eastern Nigeria, was digging a pit to use for collecting rainwater at the back of his house. In this part of the country, it is very dry for some of the year and water is usually stored during the rainy season to be used later in case of emergency. In digging the cistern, he came across a series of bronzes that were lying about two feet below the ground (nos. 15, 17, 19–24, 26–28, 30, 31, 33–35, 37, and 38). He did not know the significance of these bronzes, nor did his neighbors, but they all took pieces because they regarded them as "good medicine."

Some six months later, the British Assistant District Officer, J. O. Field, bought about forty of the pieces, published them, and then presented them to the Federal Department of Antiquities. The District Commissioner, F. W. Carpenter, also visited the site and collected most of the pieces Isaiah Anozie's neighbors had taken. Carpenter recognized the importance of these bronzes and sent them to Kenneth Murray, then the Surveyor of Antiquities in Lagos. Some were then taken to the British Museum in London for study. Murray himself subsequently visited the site and recovered more pieces, which are now in Nigerian museums. He knew the site needed to be excavated scientifically, but it was not until 1958, when the Director of the Nigerian Federal Department of Antiquities,

Bernard Fagg, persuaded Professor Thurstan Shaw to come from England to excavate, that the work was begun. Shaw worked from November 1959 to February 1960, with all objects recovered remaining the property of the Nigerian Federal Department of Antiquities.

The excavation at Igbo-Ukwu is one of the most thoroughly studied and published in the whole of Africa. Many years were spent piecing together the evidence, with extensive chemical and spectrographic analyses made of the materials themselves. The site of the original find on Isaiah Anozie's land was excavated, as well as a site in the compound of Isaiah's brother, Richard Anozie, where more bronzes were discovered. In 1964, after Shaw had joined the University of Ibadan, a third excavation was carried out in the compound of yet another brother of Isaiah Anozie, Jonah Anozie. The three sites are, therefore, referred to as Igbo Isaiah, Igbo Richard, and Igbo Jonah.

The remainder of the main group of bronzes (nos. 16, 18, 25, 29, and 32) were recovered at Igbo

Isaiah. It could be seen that originally they had lain in a rectangle very near the surface, apparently left in a small building intended to house them — possibly a shrine, but perhaps more likely a storehouse for ceremonial items (fig. 4).

The second site, known as Igbo Richard, revealed the burial chamber of an important person (fig. 5). The corpse had been seated on a stool, wearing a crown, breastplate, and bracelets, and carrying a fan and a fly whisk (no. 36). His arms were supported on metal brackets stuck into the floor of the tomb. Beside him was a staff with a head in the form of a leopard skull, while three elephant tusks lay on the ground. There were also more than ten thousand beads, some of which may have decorated his clothing. Above the ceiling of the wooden burial chamber at least five people had been sacrificially buried.

It would seem that the dead man was of great consequence. The modern Igbo do not usually have any conspicuous figures of political authority, but they do have one or two people of considerable

Figure 4 The storehouse of ritual objects uncovered at Igbo Isaiah has been reconstructed in this watercolor by Caroline Sassoon.

Figure 5 The burial chamber uncovered at Igbo Richard, reconstructed in this watercolor by Caroline Sassoon, contained a person of great importance wearing ceremonial dress and surrounded by symbols of his authority.

religious importance. One of these is the *Eze Nri*, and the site of Igbo-Ukwu lies within the area over which he has religious authority. It is his duty to ensure the continuing fertility of the soil and to help settle disputes, particularly those concerned with the title-taking system. Shaw suggested, however, that it was not an *Eze Nri* who was buried, because they have a relatively simple burial. He thought it might be an *Ozo* man, the holder of a high title whose burial does involve great pomp and ceremony.

The third site, Igbo Jonah, was an ancient pit in which had been placed a highly decorative, and therefore presumably ceremonial, pot, as well as a fine copper chain, many wristlets, six staff ornaments, and several other items.

Where and how the Igbo-Ukwu bronzes and the technique to make them entered this society is still one of the enigmas of Nigerian art history. All the objects recovered are intricately designed and made with a complete mastery of lost-wax (cire-perdue) casting. (This technique is discussed later, in Professor Willett's essay.) These bronzes are made with an alloy of copper, tin, and lead; they are, however, here referred to generally as bronzes to conform with usual practice in art history, as are the works in copper alloys found in Ife and Benin. There is no source of copper in the immediate vicinity, although tin is found in the Jos Plateau. It

is believed that the copper was traded from across the desert in North Africa, and the tin might have come from the Jos Plateau, or the copper, tin, and lead might have been already mixed in North Africa or Europe and traded down as bronze across the Sahara.

Beads were obviously of great importance in this culture; over sixty thousand of them have been found at Igbo Isaiah alone (nos. 26, 27, and 32). They have been analyzed by experts who have concluded that they resemble in composition some of the beads from Ife and probably originated in the Islamic world. These works must have been expensive items when they were made, and the people of

Igbo-Ukwu must have traded something for the materials that were used to make them. Perhaps slaves were used in exchange, or perhaps ivory, pepper, or other spices from the forest area.

Igbo-Ukwu has been dated to the ninth century A.D., but there is one date which suggests that it might have been in the fifteenth century. Shaw argued that the four radiocarbon dates for the ninth century confirmed each other and should be accepted. This early date has been challenged by Babatunde Lawal, who believes that Igbo-Ukwu could not have been earlier than the fifteenth century, first because of the state of preservation of the textiles found in association with the objects, and second because of the manillas, or bracelets, found on the site, which were introduced into West Africa as a form of currency by the Portuguese in the fifteenth century. However, there is a tradition that at that time the people living in the Niger Delta were already accustomed to finding manillas below the water and asked the Portuguese to copy them. If the ninth-century date does indeed hold up, it presents us with a new view of Africa's access to the outside world. It has often been claimed that the forest belt in West Africa was impenetrable until the arrival of the Europeans; but if this ninth-century date is firmly established, it would mean that the area was opened up to trade with both the Eastern world, on the one hand, and southern Europe on the other.

We do not really know how the culture that made these extraordinary works evolved later. Certainly, the culture of the people presently occupying this area has changed considerably. For example, there is no bronze casting being done today, but there is one similarity we can point to. Shaw thought that the incumbent of the tomb he excavated was a priest-king, someone who combined political and religious duties, and it is interesting to note that the Igbo people who inhabit this area today have no kings, but only priests. The government is carried out through a council of elders, with the head always a priest who wields some political influence as well.

IFE

Ife, or more properly Ile-Ife, has been an important city for the Yorubas for centuries. According to the most common Yoruba myth of origin, the High God Olodumare sent sixteen lesser gods to found the world and start life on its way. One of these was Oduduwa, who founded Ife and became its first King, or Oni.

It is not known exactly when what we term Ife art (nos. 39–59) began to develop, but we have radiocarbon dates for the fully developed art ranging between the eleventh and fifteenth centuries. It is interesting that the sites that have provided the significant dates have also yielded pavements made of broken pottery. Tradition has it that when a certain female Oni, Oluwo, went on an outing one rainy day, she and her regalia were splashed with mud. She was so angered by this that, on her return, she ordered the important public and religious places to be paved with potsherds. Pavements are found all over Ife and have been excavated in many places, notably at Ita Yemoo, Lafogido, Obalara's Land, and Woye Asiri. None of them, however, appear to be the paving of streets, but rather of courtyards and passageways inside buildings.

We do not know when the Ife head now in the Brooklyn Museum was discovered, but the British Museum had a plaster cast of it in their collections by 1910. The story of its travels from Ife via London to America is as yet unclear. The man who may be called the "discoverer" of Ife art is Leo Frobenius, a German ethnologist who was in Africa in the early part of this century undertaking a series of scientific expeditions. He heard that there was an ancient city where the goddess of the sea was worshiped. Knowing a great deal about ancient Greece, where the god of the sea is called Poseidon, and Rome, where he is known as Neptune, Frobenius wanted to learn more about this African god or goddess who was known as Olokun. He set out in 1910 to Ife, and in November of that year arrived and made arrangements to see the head of Olokun he had heard so much about. Learning from the people of Ife that sculptured heads were buried in the ground at the foot of giant trees and resurrected when they were required for rituals, Frobenius made arrangements with the people of Ife to go and dig where these heads were buried.

When Frobenius was shown the bronze head of Olokun, he offered to buy it for £6 plus a bottle of Scotch and a tumbler. The British district officer, Charles Partridge, heard about Frobenius's exploits, however, and he went up to Ife to stop him from exporting the head. Frobenius returned it to the owners and the £6 were returned to him. (No one knows what happened to the Scotch and the tumbler.) Frobenius did leave Nigeria with a number of terracotta heads, however, which are now in the Museum für Völkerkunde, Berlin, Federal Republic of Germany. The original "Olokun" head described by Frobenius is now represented only by a copy (fig. 6); no one knows where the original is. It is not impossible that Frobenius could have arranged for its subsequent replacement with a copy.

The next discovery of Ife material took place in 1938, when at about two hundred yards from the Palace of the Oni of Ife, a man was digging the foundation of a house in a compound called Wunmonije, and two feet below ground a hoard consisting of eighteen extraordinary bronzes was encountered (nos. 39, 40, 42, 43, 45). No one studied the site at the time, but most of the heads were kept by the Oni. Two of them (no. 42) were bought by Professor William Bascom, now Director of the Robert H. Lowie Museum of Anthropology at the University of California, Berkeley, and one was bought by a Mr. Bates, an Englishman who worked for the

Figure 6 The copy of the Ife bronze head said to represent Olokun, god of sea and wealth. It is on loan to the National Museum, Lagos, from the museum at Ife; the whereabouts of the original are unknown.

Daily Times, a newspaper owned by British interests operating in Nigeria. The two heads bought by Bascom were eventually returned to Nigeria at the instigation of the Surveyor of Antiquities, Kenneth Murray; but the head that was bought by Mr. Bates was sold to Sir Kenneth Clark (now Lord Clark), who gave it to the British Museum, where it still is.

From 1938 on, the Oni of Ife himself showed a great deal of interest in these works. When people built houses, dug in their farms, or moved earth for any purpose and came across works of art, they would take them to the Palace for safekeeping. The Oni took it upon himself to go into the shrines, the sacred groves, where the works were normally kept, and bring them into his Palace (nos. 47 and 53). These art works formed the basis of the Ife Museum for which the Oni gave land within his Palace.

The first scientific excavations to be carried out in Ife were conducted in 1949 at Abiri, although the main season was in 1953 when excavations were carried out by Bernard Fagg, William Fagg, and John Goodwin. These three men worked in the sacred groves of Osangangan Obamakin, Olokun Walode, and also at other sites. There they discovered fragments of full sculptures (no. 51), which were buried in association with other objects of more recent manufacture, leading them to conclude that these were secondary sites.

The next major excavation was undertaken in 1957, at Ita Yemoo, where a series of broken figures were recovered, one of which represents a Queen (no. 50). The original discovery of this site was accidental; workmen who were building a shed discovered a group of bronze figures (nos. 44 and 46). Frank Willett was then invited by the Federal Department of Antiquities to carry out a scientific investigation of the site, which he began during the 1957–58 season. He discovered, close by the spot where the bronzes had been found, a shrine with terracotta figures (no. 50) which probably had a mud wall and a thatched roof over it. Presumably it was burned down during hostilities. This site was quite unlike the sites of Olokun Walode and Osangangan Obamakin because it was a primary site, where things had been left by the original users. In 1962–63, another season's excavation was undertaken at Ita Yemoo and a second shrine was found over an extensive potsherd pavement (70 feet square). The first radiocarbon and thermoluminescence dates for Ife were obtained from works found at this site.

After Ita Yemoo had been excavated by Willett, a second excavation was carried out at Igbo Obameri by Oliver Myers. Here, a mound produced an assortment of terracotta heads and a curious sculpture representing a masked head. These sculptures had evidently been brought in from elsewhere and reassembled at the site; according to Myers, the process took place at the time of the return of the Ife people to Ife after its abandonment. Two such evacuations are known in the history of Ife, the first in about 1850–54 and the second in 1878–94. The radiocarbon date of the middle of the seventeenth century tends to suggest rather that the erection of the shrine was coeval with the establishment of the present dynasty by Lajamisan. In 1964, Myers again excavated a site at Oduduwa College and discovered two heads in terracotta. This site, although undated, has been claimed by Myers to be a primary site.

In 1969, I began an excavation at a site known as Odo Ogbe Street. This was undertaken after a head had been washed out by rainwater and found by two boys on their way to school early one morning (no. 48). During the excavation, we discovered that there were two archaeological deposits. At the lower level was a series of pits with round globular pots in them, and in one of the pits, a side chamber with a decayed skeleton of a human being. Unfortunately, even with emergency conservation, it was impossible to preserve it.

This particular pit had a tunnel connecting it to another pit, and it looks as if the people practiced "a pit and pot" burial. At the upper layer, a series of well-made pots was found with a few water-worn pebbles. This may have been a shrine to the goddess of the River Oshun. An interesting feature of this site is that the head was buried about two feet deep at the foot of a young tree twenty feet away from the Oshun pot complex. It appears that this head was dug up from somewhere else and used in ceremonies connected with Oshun. Because it was so precious, the head could not be left in the open, so it was buried at the foot of a tree that marked the spot.

The other site I excavated in 1969 is known as Lafogido. According to oral tradition, Lafogido was a former King of Ife, and belonged to one of the four ruling families. His compound was about two

hundred yards from the present Palace and opposite Wunmonije Compound. An earlier rescue operation had been conducted on the site in 1963 by Frank Willett, who found an elephant head (no. 55). I later excavated a mythical animal (no. 56) in the same style. Like the elephant, the mythical animal had a royal emblem on it and was placed on top of a globular pot that was inset into the edges of a rectangular pottery pavement (fig. 7). Underneath the pavement were the outlines of what could possibly be a burial site. I was so excited about the discovery that I invited the Oni to come and have a look, since he was kind enough to give permission to excavate in the first place. He came along with his chiefs, but when he saw the arrangement — about fourteen pots inserted into the edges of the pavement and five animal heads that were used as potlids — he became very agitated and decided that I should not continue with the excavation because he did not wish the bones of his ancestors to be disturbed. The Oni subsequently told Professor Willett that Lafogido was not his direct ancestor, so he had to withhold permission in order not

Figure 7 The site of Lafogido revealed a series of pots with animal-head lids arranged around a potsherd pavement that is thought to overlie a burial site.

to offend the other branch of the royal family. So that ended the excavation. A shelter has been built over it, and we must hope that it will be possible in the future to continue exploring the site.

The last two sites to be excavated in Ife were Obalara's Land and Woye Asiri, both investigated by Peter Garlake in 1971–72. Garlake uncovered a series of pavements, which confirmed that they were courtyards, in which case they can be compared to the courtyards one finds in ancient Benin. A series of very interesting terracotta sculptures was discovered. They were all taken to the University of Ife, which underwrote the excavation. (It is because the pieces are not in the National Museums that they have not been included in this exhibition.)

OWO

About eighty miles southeast of Ife lies another Yoruba town, Owo, which according to oral tradition was founded by Ojugbelu, the youngest of the sons of Oduduwa, who founded Ife. It is said that while still living in Ife, Ojugbelu went out on a hunting expedition and when he returned found that his father had split his possessions among his other children. Ojugbelu was so angry that he decided to migrate. He took with him several of the chiefs who were fond of him, and after a bit of wandering, they reached Owo, where they settled on top of a hill known as Okitisegbo. This hill is still the dominant feature of the city of Owo. We don't know exactly when this migration took place, but works excavated from Owo that probably date to the fifteenth century show clear affinities to Ife art.

The Owo excavation at the site known as Igbo'Laja was undertaken by me in 1969. The site is within a quarter of a mile of the center of the city, at the foot of the hill known as Okitisegbo, near the Olowo's Palace. Trenches were laid out and two main concentrations discovered, a primary one at the east end and a secondary at the west end (figs. 8 and 9).

The first, main concentration was found in soil that indicated that it probably was part of the mud walls of a building, while the second concentration was found in sandy soil. The obvious inference is that there was a mud house in which precious things were kept, probably with a thatched roof over it. If there was a hut housing the terracotta sculptures in the first concentration, then the second concentration was probably outside. In the second concentration, mainly broken fragments of pottery, some small sacrificial pots, iron implements, and polished stone axes were found. It looks as if this represents a place where unimportant objects that could be left out in the open, like pots, were heaped year after year. (There is a strong similarity between this arrangement and that found at shrines in Ife and at Oshogbo today, where all the important cult objects are in a mud hut, which is kept locked, whereas outside this hut, in the grove, is a series of altars with small fragments of pottery and sometimes complete pots and evidence of sacrifice here and there.) It appears that the hut was destroyed violently, because fragments from the same pieces of sculpture were discovered in widely separated areas. Fragments from one head (no. 60), for example, were found about thirteen feet apart, which tends to suggest that the work was smashed. The whole shrine might have been vandalized during a conflict between the Benin and Owo people, possibly when Benin was trying to subdue Owo in the fifteenth century.

The Owo excavations revealed works of art (nos. 60–75) that showed affinities not only to Ife art but to Benin art as well; there are also works that are in neither style. It is not clear whether the Owo objects in Ife style were brought or traded from Ife or whether they were made locally in Owo. What-

14

*Figures 8 and 9 The
excavation at Owo began
with trenches being laid out
in a box grid.*

*A later photograph (below)
of the Owo excavation site
shows how the box grid has
been converted to a trench.
Some objects can be seen in
situ.*

ever the case, the presence of the Ife style can be
clearly seen in three heads (nos. 60, 61, and 64),
while Benin motifs can be seen on three fragments
(nos. 73–75). The works in styles that had not
been seen before include two partial figures (nos.
63 and 65). Unfortunately, one of the most distinctive pieces, representing a leopard gnawing a
human leg, is too fragile to travel (fig. 34).

While we have not been able to ascertain when the
Owo people migrated from Ife, they certainly came

under the influence of Benin — a city some seventy
miles southeast of Owo — about the middle of the
fifteenth century. The Owo people claim that they
have never been conquered by the Benin people,
but there can be no doubt of the Benin influence.
The Benin Empire expanded greatly in the fifteenth century, particularly during the reign of
Ewuare, known as Ewuare the Great, and it is
doubtful whether the Owo people would have been
left alone in this process, which resulted in the
empire being stretched as far as the present border

15

of the Republic of Benin, formerly Dahomey. The dating for the Owo material seems to confirm the Benin influence. The excavation revealed a date of A.D. 1435 ±65, and it was in the middle of the fifteenth century that the Benin Empire was expanded to the east and west. In any case, there is a great deal of similarity between Owo and Benin, not only in the works of art but in the nature of the architecture. For example, corrugated walls are used in both Benin and Owo. There are also certain chieftaincy titles used in Owo that are obviously derived from Benin. Even the regalia of the Olowo is closely related to that of the Oba of Benin (figs. 10 and 36). The Olowo's crown is made not of the multicolored trade beads usual for Yoruba kings but of the same kind of coral beads as are used for the crown of the Oba of Benin. The high collar and projections on the crown show that

the Benin Late Period heads are not exaggerated (fig. 35).

How can we describe what happened to this art? There is one head into which the Owo people had drilled a hole so they could use it as a pendant, just as people in Benin wear pendants. The priest of the sacred grove known as Igbo'Laja was so excited when we discovered this object that he went back into his grove and brought out another head (fig. 11 and no. 61), which also had a hole drilled into the forehead, a hole fresher than the head itself, which is greatly abraded. Both these examples suggest that the art came to an end and that the sculptures were then reused in secondary or modern contexts. Another fascinating piece of evidence supporting this theory was found at the site of the excavation. In the middle of the main concentration was a piece of charred wood, and underneath was a hole with two fragments of terracotta sculptures buried in it. The carbon material taken from this hole or pit yielded a date in the seventeenth century. The Owo people had probably discovered the fragments of sculpture while digging in the ground and used them in a modern context. Afterward they reburied them in this pit, not knowing what else lay there, and used charred wood to mark where the pit was dug. (This form of marking was also used in Odo Ogbe Street in Ife.) These two instances seem to confirm the observation first made by Leo Frobenius in 1910 that classical works of art are reburied by present-day

Figure 10 The regalia of the Olowo (King) of Owo, as seen in this photograph taken in 1909, is closely related to that of the Oba of Benin (fig. 36).

16

Figure 11 The present-day Alaja (priest) of Igbo'Laja is seen here wearing a pendent head (no. 61).

people, who dig them up and use them in rituals, then rebury them in places where they can be unearthed for future rituals.

BENIN

According to the Benin historian Chief Jacob Egharevba, the Edo-speaking Benin people claim in their oral traditions to have come from the skies. Some historians say they came from Sudan, some say they are related to the Ife people. Most scholars accept Egharevba's suggestion that the Benin dynasty under whose rule the works of art in this exhibition were produced was established from Ife.

The original Benin people had an institution of kingship that probably differed from the present one. The name usually given to the rulers of the first dynasty in Benin is Ogiso. About the twelfth century, the Benin people had a succession problem among themselves, and invited an outsider to come and rule over them. This outsider was Oranmiyan, son of the founder of the Yoruba Kingdom of Ife, Oduduwa. It is said that Oduduwa did not trust the Benin people to look after his son properly, and so to test their devotion, he sent seven lice to be cared for. The Benin people looked after these little creatures for seven years, and then returned them to Oduduwa, who, convinced that the Benin people were now careful enough, sent his son Oranmiyan to rule over them. Oranmiyan went to Benin and married Erinmwide, the daughter of the Onogie of Ego; as a result, a son was born who was named Eweka. Oranmiyan eventually left Benin and returned to Ife, and his son Eweka was made the King of Benin, becoming Eweka I. The present Oba, Oba Erediuwa I, is thirty-ninth in the line of succession in this dynasty.

Oral tradition has it that it was during the reign of Oguola, the sixth Oba of Benin in the late fourteenth century, that bronze casters were requested to be sent from Ife. There are many arguments for and against this theory, which will not be gone into here. However, it is generally believed that it was during the reign of Oguola that bronze casting started in Benin, and it is from this period that we have the beginning of the corpus of bronze memorial heads (nos. 76 and 77).

The Benin political organization is such that the Oba, or King, has always been a very rich man. Tribute was paid to the King from all over his empire, which was very wide. The people of Benin, known as the Bini, had a monopoly of trade with the Portuguese, who first made contact in 1485, as well as with other European nations. The Oba was so rich that he was able to maintain a specialist guild of bronze casters who were responsible for making the bronzes, owned exclusively by the King himself and stored in his Palace. The bronze casters were forbidden on pain of death to make these bronzes for anybody except the King, who could as a mark of favor, of course, give some pieces to those whom he chose to honor. There were other guilds, as well, for ivory carving, wood carving, and so on.

The Benin Empire produced brass castings and ivory carvings for several centuries (nos. 76–91). There seem to have been two periods of particular importance: first, in the reign of Esigie (c. 1550), when brass supplied by the European traders became plentiful and new forms such as Queen Mother heads (no. 76) were introduced; and second, in the reign of Eresonye (c. 1735–50), when brass became even more plentiful and new forms again appeared.

The art of Benin continued to evolve up to 1897. In that year, the British Vice-Consul, J. R. Philips, sent a message to the King of Benin saying that he wished to visit him. The Oba in reply asked him not to come then, as he would be engaged with the year's most important ceremony, the Igue, a time when the King's body is sacred and he becomes a divine person. The ceremony is performed to ensure the continuity of the dynasty and the welfare of the entire Empire. Philips decided to set out nevertheless. Without the knowledge of the King, two of his chiefs arranged an ambush, killing all

except two of the European members of the expedition and all their porters. The two who escaped raised the alarm and a naval expedition was mounted very quickly.

The King of Benin was horrified at the massacre and afraid of what the consequences might be. The oracle was consulted and prophesied that the town would be destroyed at the hands of white men. The people of Benin had to take steps to safeguard their city, which included a number of sacrifices to the gods to stave off the imminent disaster. When the European troops entered the city and found large numbers of human victims, they thought this represented the traditional way of Benin life. After subduing the town, they removed about two thousand antiquities that were concentrated in the Palace (fig. 12). These were sold off by the British government to help defray the costs of the expedition. The King was deposed and subsequently exiled. This Punitive Expedition thus effectively brought an end to traditional Benin art.

A number of the plaques taken out by the British were presented to the British Museum, and more pieces were purchased at the sales. Some of the plaques were subsequently sold to the National Museum in Lagos. The great bulk of Benin art, however, is scattered throughout museums and private collections all over the world. Since World War II, the Nigerian government has made a great effort to recover as much Benin art as possible, but although Nigeria now holds the third largest collection in the world (after those in the British Museum and in Berlin), it is small in number for a country that produced such a large body of work. When the National Museum in Benin opened a few years back, an appeal was made on the platform of the International Council of Museums to give long-term loans, or to return one or two pieces to Benin City itself, so that the work their ancestors made could be shown in this museum. Unfortunately,

Figure 12 British soldiers sit surrounded by Benin works of art during the Punitive Expedition of 1897.

although the resolution was adopted and an appeal sent out, there was no response from anywhere in the world. Benin is now left to show remnants and second-rate objects, as well as casts and photographs of pieces that once belonged to them. Perhaps it is time that the circumstances in which these objects were removed from Benin should be looked at again. Museums that have acquired the works of art could lend one object, maybe two, and if these are collected from several sources, perhaps Benin Museum itself would be able to show Benin works in their proper context.

THE TSOEDE BRONZES

In a village on the Island of Jebba and in the village of Tada on the bank of the River Niger there used to be two groups of bronzes that are usually referred to as the Tsoede bronzes (nos. 92–96 and figs. 13 and 14). Tsoede is the legendary founder of the Nupe Kingdom and tradition has it that he was a ward of the court of the Ata (King) of Idah. It is said that he escaped, taking these bronzes with him, and sailed up the River Niger in a bronze canoe, depositing some of the sculpture at Tada

and some at Jebba. He then went on to found the Nupe Kingdom. These events are supposed to have taken place in the sixteenth century.

The bronzes total nine in number. There is a seated figure from Tada (no. 92) in Ife style that must be considered all by itself. Then there are four works that share certain common stylistic characteristics: two Jebba figures, the bowman (no. 94), which is male, and a female figure (fig. 14), which was stolen from the island early in the 1970s; and two Tada works, a warrior (no. 93) and a male figure with a staff (no. 95). There is also a bronze figure with clasped hands (no. 96) that is not unlike modern Yoruba sculpture. Finally, there is a group of three animal figures in bronze, the style of which

has not yet been related to any previously recorded bronze tradition.

Although it appears that the bowman is related to the Benin tradition and the seated figure is in the Ife tradition, there are many unanswered questions concerning these two works, as well as the other Tsoede bronzes. Was it a coincidence that the three largest bronzes we find in Africa (nos. 93 and 94 and fig. 14) should all be in one small area? Is there no other tradition that could have produced them? If one looks at the Benin corpus, there really is nothing comparable to them. The same observation applies, to a lesser degree, to the seated bronze figure, although it exhibits Ife affinities. Could there not have been another tradition that made this bronze in Ife style? These are some of

Figure 13 The Tsoede bronzes, three of which are shown here (nos. 92, 95, and 96), are a mysterious group of bronzes found in the small village of Tada on the bank of the River Niger and on the Island of Jebba (opposite page).

Figure 14 This female figure from the Island of Jebba in the River Niger is a companion piece to the Jebba bowman (no. 94). Its whereabouts are at present unknown (left).

the questions art historians, archaeologists, and anthropologists will have to ask themselves as they deal with this material in the future.

ESIE SOAPSTONE FIGURES

The Esie soapstone figures (nos. 98 and 99) are the largest collection of stone carvings still in Africa. More than eight hundred of them have been found, ranging from 14 cm. to over 1 meter. These carved figures, presided over by a "King," represent men and women, some playing musical instruments and many armed with machetes. Every year, throughout the reigns of fifteen chiefs of Esie, there has been a festival for the images. Also, at various times throughout the year, supplications accompanied by sacrifices are presented to the images

through the *Aworo*, or Chief Priest (fig. 15). Esie tradition holds that the statues are the petrified remains of visitors from a distant land. They are, in fact, as much a mystery to the Esie people as they are to the rest of the world. The Esie people probably arrived in their present location at the end of the eighteenth century to find these figures already there.

H. G. Ramsey, schools inspector for the Church Missionary Society, is credited with the "discovery" of the soapstone figures in 1933, although Leo Frobenius had collected three heads in Esie style as early as 1912. In 1945, a House of Images was built to protect the figures, but it had begun to decay by the early 1960s. A young Peace Corps volunteer named Phillips Stevens, Jr., was engaged by Kenneth Murray during 1965–66 to

Figure 15 The Chief Priest, or Aworo, prostrates himself before the "King of the Images" in the grove where the Esie soapstone figures were originally found.

photograph and catalogue the collection while a new group of buildings was constructed for the works. The Esie Museum officially opened in 1970, with an altar that the people use in their worship of the images.

IKOM MONOLITHS

The Ikom monoliths (fig. 16 and no. 100) are a group of some three hundred mysterious sculptures located in an area northeast of the village of Ikom occupied by five subgroups of the northern Ekoi. These anthropomorphic stone pillars range in height from a little under 1 meter to a little over 1.5 meters. No archaeological excavations have yet taken place in the area, although one is being planned. It would be highly desirable in order to

provide an authentic context for these intriguing works, which at the moment are surrounded by more legend than fact.

Most of the sculptures presented in this catalogue are treasures dug up from the earth, either accidentally or through scientific excavations. In spite of the fact that archaeological research in Nigeria is still in its infancy and the fact that many works have been lost through ignorance, what is presented here is enough to provide us with a broad insight into the life and times of the ancient people who occupied the present political area called Nigeria and to prove that those who hold that Africa has no history are wrong.

It has often been suggested that the high arts of Nigeria, namely those of Ife and Benin, were made by itinerant European artists or were stimulated by

22

outside influences. This misconception, although it has greatly abated, still lingers on. This exhibition should finally end the controversy. No one has yet suggested — nor is there any evidence for it — that any part of Nigeria had been in contact with Europe as early as the first millennium B.C. when the Nok sculptures were being made. So far, too, no one has suggested that the Nok sculptures were the works of outsiders or influenced from the outside. If it is agreed then that the Nok sculptures were made by Africans, there is no reason to think that a thousand years later, the Ife people and a little later, the Bini, could not on their own have produced the works that today are seen to be among the world's great art treasures. In any case, the scientific dates now calculated for these works confirm that the traditions developed indigenously before the first European contacts were made in the late fifteenth century.

But more research is needed. Archaeologically, the work has barely started; there is ample evidence to lead us to believe that the gaps in the history of our cultural and artistic development can be filled. The world would be greatly enriched by this knowledge. It is, perhaps, appropriate to recall the words of the famous archaeologist Sir Mortimer Wheeler, who wrote in the Preface to Professor Willett's book *Ife in the History of West African Sculpture:* "When the new Africa finds the moment and the mood for the discovery of its own past, here are matters which, properly understood, will provide a new chapter to world history." Let me conclude by adding that these are works which, when properly understood, will not only provide a new chapter to world history but also restore the dignity of man in Africa and wherever people of African descent are dispersed.

Figure 16 These typical Cross River monoliths (akwanshi) are seen here in their original setting at Agba.

NIGERIAN ART: AN OVERVIEW

FRANK WILLETT

NIGERIA is a country whose boundaries were given to it in the days of the British Empire and, hence, its lines are essentially artificial, often cutting in two the territories occupied by peoples living along its frontiers. Nevertheless, during the colonial period (1884/5–1960), there flourished in Nigeria an extraordinary number of sculptural traditions, more than in any other area of Africa. Under the leadership of Kenneth Murray, first Director of the Federal Department of Antiquities, steps were taken in colonial times to protect Nigeria's artistic heritage and to explore its past. Dr. Ekpo Eyo, Guest Curator of this exhibition, is the first Nigerian successor to Kenneth Murray and has himself contributed greatly to our knowledge of the history of sculpture in Nigeria.

The richness of Nigeria's recent sculptural styles is rooted in ancient artistic traditions. We have more information about ancient sculpture from Nigeria than from any other part of the continent. This may, in part, be due to the fact that considerable effort has been expended in the study of the art history, but it does also seem to reflect a reality — that from at least as early as the mid-first millennium B.C., what we nowadays know as Nigeria was the home of a succession of artistic styles of great importance. We can speak of a succession, for we can assign dates to them, though the history of Nigerian sculpture is still episodic in character. We can identify some of the high-water marks of artistic achievement, but the connection of one to another is not always as clear as we might wish. A good deal of the evidence almost certainly consisted of sculpture in wood that has not survived, and its stylistic features may not necessarily be reflected in the sculptures in durable materials that have survived.

This exhibition illustrates some of the more important works from the main artistic traditions: Nok, Igbo-Ukwu, Ife, Owo, and Benin. Of these, Nok, Ife, Owo, Benin, and the Tsoede bronzes seem to be linked, while other traditions — Igbo-Ukwu,

Esie, and Ikom — seem at present to be isolated in time and space. It is hoped that continuing research will one day reveal their ancestors and descendants.

Before one can satisfactorily study the history of art in a country as vast as Nigeria, one needs to establish a chronology. In the past twenty-five years, two techniques have been applied, radiocarbon and thermoluminescence, which have greatly helped archaeologists and art historians in their efforts to date undocumented materials.

The radiocarbon dating system depends basically on the very accurate measurement of two forms, or isotopes, of carbon, carbon 12, which is inert, and carbon 14, which is radioactive. All living things are composed in large measure of carbon in a fixed proportion of radioactive to inert forms. When a living being dies, its radioactive carbon begins to decay. It takes 5,730 years for half of the radioactive carbon to decay; this is called the half-life of carbon 14. It is thus possible to estimate how long ago the organism died by measuring what proportion of carbon 14 is left in a sample of, say, charcoal. Unfortunately, radioactive decay does not go on steadily, but rather proceeds in fits and starts. Consequently, a series of measurements, usually about ten, are taken on each sample and the results are calculated statistically. The date is quoted with a "Standard Deviation" to indicate the limits within which there is a two-to-one chance that the date lies. A date of A.D. 1435 ± 95 would thus have a two-to-one chance of lying somewhere between A.D. 1340 and A.D. 1530, but it could be anywhere between those dates.

Radiocarbon dates are obtained from organic remains found with human artifacts. Their reliability depends on the precision with which the organic material can be associated with the artifacts. In contrast, thermoluminescence dates are derived directly from the clay of which terracotta

sculptures are made or from the clay of the core inside a bronze casting. Thermoluminescence depends on the fact that minerals in clay can trap energy in their crystal lattice. This is discharged when the clay is fired to make a pot or a sculpture. The object then begins to collect energy again, in part from radioactivity within the clay itself and in part from the environment around it. This accumulated energy can only be measured once, and complicated estimates need to be made of the relative importance of the different sources of the energy and of the moisture of the environment in the past.

Although there are uncertainties in each of these dating techniques, they have been of enormous help. Since the first radiocarbon dates for Nigerian objects were obtained in 1957, considerable effort has been put into establishing a chronology for Nigeria's cultures, and now there are scores of dates from thermoluminescence as well as radiocarbon, which have provided the general sequence outlined in this catalogue. Because of the uncertainties, however, we have usually expressed the dates in general terms rather than citing them precisely.

NOK, located off the edge of the Jos plateau, is a small mining village where the earliest sculptures found so far in Nigeria were discovered. The Nok culture flourished from at least as early as the middle of the first millennium B.C. until around the middle of the first millennium A.D. There are other traditions of terracotta sculpture found during the last few years, which show changes in style but seem to be continuing much of the Nok tradition into the late first millennium A.D. (no. 14 and fig. 27).

The people of Nok sculpted terracotta, a word that artists often use for pottery sculpture — there is no necessary technical difference between terracotta and pottery. They were highly skilled in this art, making sculptures of full-length human figures that must have been 4 feet or more in height. The largest head so far published from Nok (no. 1) is over 14 inches in height, and even if the head were a quarter of the overall height of the figure, as is usual in African sculpture, that would suggest that the figure must have been 4 feet tall. Making such large terracotta figures is a very unusual skill. The sculptors were able to fire them successfully, an extremely difficult task in an uncontrolled, open fire. There is no real evidence that they fired them in kilns, although because they were skilled in the use of furnaces to make iron, it is possible that they may have had some sort of kiln. They took great care in modeling to keep the thickness of the sculpture even. When there is a heavy collar of beads around the neck, as in number 1, the tubular section has been left hollow. If it had been made solid, the moisture in the clay might have caused it to explode when being fired.

There are several characteristics that distinguish the Nok style (fig. 17). Perhaps most noticeable is the treatment of the eyes, which form either a segment of a circle or sometimes a rather triangular form, with the eyebrow above balancing the sweep of the lower lid, sometimes making a circle. The second distinguishing feature is that the pupils of the eyes, the nostrils, the lips, and the ears are normally pierced through the clay. A third feature is that the ears are located on the head in rather

strange places, at the angle of the jaw, or even on the back of the head.

The Nok people almost certainly also carved in wood, although none of the wood carvings have survived. The technique of sculpting in terracotta is additive, that is to say, pieces are added on and usually smoothed into the work already done, whereas wood carving is a subtractive technique, taking away from the block bits that are not wanted. In carving wood, the artist blocks out the main forms before refining them. Some of the Nok terracottas have retained the forms of blocked-out shapes, which must derive from wood sculpture (fig. 26). The way in which the surface detail is incised on the terracotta also often appears to be carried over from wood carving. It may well be that the striking similarities we often see between the eyes of modern Yoruba wood sculptures (especially

Figure 17 This head (no. 2) exhibits typical Nok features: eyes that form a segment of a circle, with the eyebrow above balancing the sweep of the lower lid; pierced eyes, nostrils, and ears (in this case not the mouth); a pointed beard; and carefully represented hairstyle.

gelede masks) and those of Nok terracotta sculptures represent a real continuity of more than two and a half millennia.

We cannot be sure, but we may reasonably suppose that like recent African societies, the people who made these sculptures practiced some form of ancestor cult and believed in witchcraft. The high degree of artistic skill of the sculptures suggests that the artists could have made naturalistic sculptures if they wished. Indeed, some of the animal sculptures represent their subject matter in a fairly realistic way. There must have been a strong reason not to represent human beings in a realistic manner, too. It may have been the belief in witchcraft that caused this, for recent African artists have declared that they avoid making recognizable likenesses of living individuals for fear of being accused of witchcraft.

Many of the finest Nok pieces are human heads that have been broken from full figures. Their form tends to be basically geometric, either cylindrical (nos. 1 and 5), conical (nos. 2, 3, and 7), or spherical (nos. 4 and 8). One of the most famous pieces in the exhibition (no. 1) is a highly conceptualized representation of a human head, and yet it has a great vitality about it, a vivid expression of life about the eyes, which have been very carefully modeled. It also shows very clearly the interest taken by the Nok artists in the careful representation of elaborate hairstyles. In this case the hair is dressed into a large number of buns with a small hole in the top of each, probably intended to hold a

feather. A similar hairstyle is still used among the Kachichiri and Numana who live only about thirty miles east of Nok. Of course, this style of hairdressing may not have continued in use all this time. It probably disappeared and then was reinvented; as with any fashion, reversions to older styles occur from time to time. Several Nok pieces have a hairdressing with locks on the side of the head (fig. 17, nos. 2 and 3) which is later echoed in some of the Ife sculptures as well. The rings representing the curls of hair seen on figure 17 (no. 2) are found also on sculpture from Ife (fig. 18).

One of the most intriguing heads (no. 8) has its cheeks remarkably puffed up, with the lips pushed forward, but it is difficult to tell precisely what this

Figure 18 This Ife sculpture shows the hair represented by a similar convention to that seen on the Nok head in figure 17.

indicates. I have seen musicians playing reeded instruments and puffing out their cheeks in a similar way, and this may perhaps be what is represented here, though there is no indication of any instrument; moreover, the lips do not have the opening usually found on Nok heads.

Nok figures are also characterized by their profusion of beads. Even the foot in the exhibition (no. 11), striking for its size, wears a great number of anklets. One can see particularly clearly in the three small full-length figures (nos. 9, 10, and 12) a whole arrangement of beads around the body, particularly the thick beaded collar, and the ropes of beads that hang around the chest and abdomen.

The Nok artistic style changed with time. Recent discoveries at three or four sites in northern Nigeria have shown that there were traditions of sculpture in terracotta continuing throughout most of the first millennium A.D. (no. 14 and fig. 27). Some works, for example the human figure from Yelwa in this exhibition (no. 14), appear to show the decline of the Nok style. By this time, the late first millennium A.D., there were two separate traditions to the south: that of Igbo-Ukwu, with a metalworking art flourishing around the ninth century A.D.; and Ife, occupied by the ninth century, although the earliest sculpture is probably only from the eleventh or twelfth.

IGBO-UKWU is a small village in southeastern Nigeria in the area occupied nowadays by the Igbo, and we may assume that the people who made these elaborate metal castings (nos. 15–38) were ancestors of the present people. The sculpture is dated by five radiocarbon dates, four from the ninth to tenth centuries and one from the fourteenth to fifteenth. In several cases, well-preserved fabric was found surrounding the castings, which has led Babatunde Lawal to argue in favor of the later date. However, the presence of copper in the ground with the fabric would have inhibited bacterial decay and have allowed the cloth to be preserved. It seems to me that the weight of evidence favors the four early dates.

The early dating means that the people of Igbo-Ukwu were the earliest workers of copper and its alloys in West Africa. Moreover, they knew that copper was not suitable for casting, so they worked it by smithing (nos. 29 and 30), whilst for castings they used leaded bronze, which flows better in enclosed molds (nos. 15–28 and 31–38). These metals were probably imported, like the beads, from far away. Thurstan Shaw, the excavator of Igbo-Ukwu, suggests that ivory, slaves, and perhaps kola nuts were traded in exchange. Such a concentration of wealth as the metalwork and the beads represent has been thought to imply some sort of centralized government unlike the stateless societies that characterized Igboland at the time of the first European contacts. This point is discussed in Dr. Eyo's Introduction and need not be pursued here.

The style of the art is most unusual; in fact, it is unique in the corpus of African art. We know nothing of where it came from and almost nothing of what it led to later. There is nothing much similar in the area today, though we can find some parallels of minor detail in more recent works. The art arose, flourished, and seems to have disappeared.

Its outstanding feature is the great elaboration of the surface decoration: the objects have an encrusted appearance. Most conspicuous are the number of small animals, especially insects, which stand out from the surface. Tiny spirals are also commonly employed. Even repairs to faults in the castings were made in the form of spirals. Other decorations were formed of long fine threads, which may be run in straight lines or used to outline other shapes, particularly rectangles or lozenges, or to form networks of various types, either triangular or curvilinear. One characteristic form, seen very clearly on two vessels (nos. 15 and 19), consists of a series of straight lines forming lozenge shapes with pairs of rings or holes in the center and the remainder of the background covered with tiny pellets. There may also be a boss or a loop at each corner of the lozenge. The bowl mentioned above (no. 19) also shows another characteristic motif, a very stylized floral pattern.

Most of the metal objects in this exhibition were made by the cire-perdue or lost-wax process of casting. In this process, the object to be cast is modeled in beeswax, over a clay core if the casting is to be hollow, in which case metal pins or chaplets are pushed through the wax into the core to hold it in position in the later stages. The beeswax is sculpted, and extra strips of wax are applied to an inconspicuous part of the work. The object is then coated first with fine clay and then with coarser clay; the ends of the extra strips of wax are left uncovered. The entire mold is then baked hard in a fire, the molten wax being poured out into a bowl of water (so it can be used again) through the holes formed in the mold by the extra strips of wax. Next, molten metal is poured into the hot mold through the holes to fill the void left by the wax. These holes, called runners, are partly filled with metal. The outer part of the mold is broken off and the metal that filled the runners is cut off, along with the ends of the pins that held the core in place. If it is accessible, the clay core is broken into pieces and removed.

The Igbo-Ukwu artists were exceptionally skilled bronze casters and a number of their castings were made in stages. One vessel on a base (no. 15), for example, was initially made in two sections, the bowl on its own pedestal foot above the first row of rectangular holes and the base below these holes.

The two sections were then joined together by casting on the rectangular strips decorated with insects and openwork spiral forms. It seems that the insects and spiral decorations were cast separately beforehand and placed in the wax model before it was invested in clay.

A second vessel (no. 16), shaped like an elongated globular pot on a base, was also made by a very complicated procedure. The body of the vessel and the upper part of the stand seem to have been made as a single casting. The neck of the pot, the lower part of the stand, and the ropework cage without the bottom loops were cast separately, one loop of the rope being passed through a separate cast decoration. The ropework was passed over the pot from above and bent to fit. The rim was attached to the body of the pot by casting on more metal to join them. This was done also to join the two parts of the base together, the lower loops of the ropework cage being added in this same stage of the casting. One can only suppose that the smiths of Igbo-Ukwu enjoyed demonstrating their virtuosity.

There are a number of vessels (nos. 17–21) that are made now of bronze but that represent originals made from calabashes, or gourds, which have been cut in half and had a handle of metal fitted on the outside (fig. 19). During his excavation, Shaw found metal handles for calabashes, and in at least one case part of the calabash itself had survived. The larger bowls (nos. 17–19), which have handles only on one side, must have been very awkward to use. This, together with the very great surface enrichment, leads to the conclusion that their use was ritual rather than functional.

The bowls made from smaller calabashes (nos. 20 and 21) were cut across in the opposite way to the larger ones. These may have been used as drinking cups, for certainly small calabashes cut in this way

Figure 19 A number of vessels from Igbo-Ukwu, including this one (no. 21), are based on the shape of a calabash or gourd (nos. 17—22).

are used nowadays in men's societies for drinking palm-wine. A small dipper (no. 24) is quite similar, but the handle is on one end and the opposite end is distinctly pointed and would have served as a spout. Many of these vessels have spiral bosses close to the handle (nos. 20, 21, and 24) and sometimes others on the opposite side from the handle (nos. 17 and 19.) These were made of coiled wire in the original calabash vessels but are part of the casting in these copies. While they serve as decoration in some cases, it is possible that they sometimes afforded a grip for the second hand (nos. 17 and 19).

A number of other castings from this site are also thought to have served as vessels in ceremonies. Two of the most beautiful are based on shells,

probably representing the seashell Triton, one decorated with flies and frogs (no. 22), and the other decorated with the very stylized representation of a leopard (no. 23).

A number of works from Igbo-Ukwu are fittings for ceremonial staffs (nos. 25—30). One of them still has, in the center, the remains of an iron spike by which it was attached to the top of a staff (no. 25). Two of these staff ornaments (nos. 26 and 27) also retain some of the beads that were strung through loops in the casting; originally they were extensively covered with beads. Two ornaments seem to have been intended to fit in the central part of a staff, since the aperture goes right through (nos. 27 and 28), while two others seem to have come from the top or bottom end (nos. 29 and 30) of staffs.

Three sites were excavated at Igbo-Ukwu: a storehouse filled with ritual objects (fig. 4), a grave of an important personage (fig. 5), and a pit. Most of the objects in this exhibition were from the storehouse. Of the objects found in the grave, most were made from copper by smithing, but one, the handle of a fly whisk, was made by casting (no. 36). Fly whisks are widely used in Africa as an emblem of authority. This one was probably lying across the lap of the body in the grave. The person was buried sitting on a stool and surrounded by various symbols of his authority. This fly whisk would have had animal hairs attached to the bottom end of it but these, of course, did not survive to be excavated.

The fly whisk is also an important piece because of its representation of a human being. Although African art is usually interested in the representation of the human form, such representations are rare at Igbo-Ukwu. Both examples in this exhibition (nos. 31 and 36) show a scarification pattern radiating from the bridge of the nose. This scarification, although superficially resembling that of Ife, does not seem to be linked to it. It does, however, have some resemblance to the *itchi* scarification, which is used as a mark of high achievement among modern Igbo men.

The second human representation is one of a group of pendants (nos. 31–34). These were probably part of the ceremonial costume and used in a similar way to masks still worn on the hips of chiefs in Benin City. In addition to the human head, there is one pendant that represents a bird brooding over two eggs, which are themselves covered with flies (no. 32), one a ram (no. 33), and one an elephant (no. 34). From the back of the bird and eggs pendant hang chains of wire decorated with beads, on the ends of which are small castings that would have jingled when it was worn. The other works in this group would have been decorated in the same

way, for they too are provided with little loops for the attachment of similar chains.

IFE lies on the opposite side of the River Niger from Igbo-Ukwu in southwestern Nigeria in the area occupied by the Yoruba people, who number about ten million. According to their traditions, Ife is the center where the gods descended from heaven on an iron chain to create and populate the world. Oduduwa made the world and was its first ruler. His children spread out to found their own kingdoms throughout what we now know as Yorubaland. These kings and their successors consequently were and still are regarded as being semidivine.

We know from radiocarbon dates obtained from excavations that Ife existed from about A.D. 800, and perhaps two centuries before that. Several sites have been excavated in Ife, and though some, like Lafogido and Odo Ogbe Street (nos. 48, 55, and 56) have only produced single dates, they correspond to the dates from other sites where longer series of dates are available, such as Ita Yemoo (nos. 44, 46, and 50), Obalara's Land, and Woye Asiri. These indicate, after calibration, that the naturalistic "Classical" art of Ife flourished from the eleventh or twelfth centuries into the fourteenth or fifteenth. Two radiocarbon dates have been obtained from sites in which older sculptures of the Classical period had been reused (no. 48). These are of the sixteenth and seventeenth centuries, suggesting that these sculptures had ceased to be made by that time. Some Ife sculptures that show a progression from the naturalism of Classical Ife art toward the stylization of modern Yoruba sculpture are thought to date from about this same period and are thus described as "post-Classical" (fig. 31).

The art of Ife is unique in Africa in representing human beings with a realism that makes them almost portraitlike in appearance. The art is of such a high quality that it has often been compared with the other great naturalistic traditions — those of Ancient Greece and Rome and of the European Renaissance — as well as with the rather more stylized art of Dynastic Egypt. Such comparisons greatly obscured our understanding of the art of Ife, which used to be interpreted as being in some way an artistic colony of one or another of these traditions. The scientific dates have ruled out all these possible sources, and today we can see the art of Ife as one of the high-water marks of truly African artistic achievement.

About thirty of the sculptures are cast in metal, either copper or zinc brass. Copper is not suitable for casting by pouring into an enclosed mold because it oxidizes quickly on contact with the air and will not flow well. If tin, zinc, or lead are added, the metal flows well without the same degree of oxidation. The Igbo-Ukwu smiths were aware of this difference in working quality between copper and its alloys, so they used smithing techniques — hammering, twisting, bending, and incising — on copper (nos. 29 and 30), but for the castings (nos. 15–28, and 31–38), they used mainly leaded bronze — i.e., copper with a little tin and more lead. The Ife smiths, however, managed to cast successfully in copper. The "Obalufon" mask (no. 41) is a flawless casting in copper, and five of the heads from Wunmonije Compound (including no. 43) were also cast in copper. This was probably done by sealing the mold onto the crucible containing the metal, heating the crucible until the metal melted, then inverting the whole assemblage so that the metal could run into the mold with no contact with the outside air. The seated figure of Tada (no. 92) is probably the work of an Ife smith. This, too, was cast in copper, but less successfully, presumably because the large size made it impossible to use this technique, the combined mold, crucible, and metal being too heavy and awkward to

handle. Instead, the metal appears to have been poured from open crucibles, with the result that it failed to run properly into the mold and at least twenty areas had to be made good by burnt-in repairs (sometimes called casting on). This involved remodeling the missing parts in wax, providing runners for each repair, investing it in clay again, and repeating the whole casting process. The thermoluminescence date from the seated figure of Tada, of the early fourteenth century, is the earliest direct date we have from any of the Ife castings. It may well be that at the time they had not learned how to avoid this difficulty.

The other Ife castings are made of an alloy of zinc, lead, and copper. Alloys of copper and tin or copper and lead are called bronzes, whereas those in which zinc is the main addition to the copper are called brasses. It is not possible to tell whether a casting is made of bronze or of brass other than by some form of scientific examination, so art historians usually lump all such castings together as "bronzes." We use the term "bronze" in this book in this same generalized way; but where the object has been analyzed, we have indicated its composition in a more precise way, for example, as a zinc brass or a leaded bronze. It is interesting to note that the metal used at Ife was quite different in composition from that used at Igbo-Ukwu. The small amounts of other elements in the copper show that their copper came from different sources, though we cannot yet state exactly where.

None of the Ife castings was found in a context which could be dated by radiocarbon, but the thermoluminescence dates indicate that they are later than many of the terracottas dated by both techniques. It seems that the art of Ife developed in terracotta and was translated into metal as a fully developed art style at the time when knowledge of the technique of casting was introduced to the area.

The subject matter of the art consists mainly of royal figures and their attendants, probably reflecting the political structure of ancient Ife as a city-state ruled over by a King or Oni. Although from the sixteenth or seventeenth century onward the importance of Ife in Yorubaland as a whole seems to have been restricted to the religious sphere, in earlier times it seems to have held widespread political influence over the kingdoms founded by the sons of Oduduwa. Their tribute no doubt furnished the people of Ife with the resources to buy the metal for the castings, which appears to have been carried across the desert from North Africa, if not all the way from Europe. Glass beads used in the ceremonial costumes seem to have been imported from both northern Europe and the Islamic Near East. Around the sixteenth and seventeenth centuries, these supplies seem to have ceased as the tributary kingdoms asserted their independence from Ife, ceasing to pay tribute and interrupting the trade. Bronze casting was brought to an end, though terracotta sculpture continued since the materials were available locally; but the style changed to become increasingly stylized (fig. 31).

Most of the known Ife castings are lifesize heads. Three in this catalogue (nos. 39, 40, and 43) are from a group that were found at Wunmonije Compound in 1938 and 1939 along with two heads with crowns (no. 42) and the broken figure (no. 45). The three crowned heads are smaller than life size (fig. 6 and no. 42). It seems likely, therefore, that the other heads were intended to carry real crowns, since they are of life size and have holes for the attachment of the crown. The area at the top of the head that the holes demarcate has been either built up (nos. 40 and 43) or cut back (no. 39) in order to fit the crown. It seems then that these heads, which have holes in the neck, were intended for attachment to a wooden body and to carry the crown of the dead King in a second burial cere-

mony, very similar to the second burial ceremonies that were conducted for the Kings of England and later of France in the later Middle Ages. So far as we can tell, these ceremonies were independently invented more or less simultaneously in Britain and Ife. In both cases, the purpose was to show that although the King was dead, the power of the office continued, an idea that is still expressed in the phrase used on the death of the King of England: The King is dead, long live the King.

The function of the mask (no. 41) is not at all certain. Cast of unalloyed copper, it is clearly intended to be worn as a mask and is remarkable because pure copper is particularly difficult to cast, yet this is a flawless casting. Whether it was used to impersonate someone during the burial ceremonies, or at some subsequent event, we simply do not know, and it seems unprofitable to guess. This piece is supposed to have been kept on an altar in the Palace in Ife ever since it was made. It has been given the name of the Oni Obalufon, who is credited with having introduced the art of casting into Ife; however, there is no other evidence that it does represent him.

There are also full-length figures from Ife representing Kings (nos. 44 and 45) and Queens (no. 46). They wear a similar costume whatever their sex: a heavy beaded collar around the neck, finer necklaces covering the chest, a heavier rope of beads around the outer edge of the trunk; while in the center of the chest there hangs a double bow, which seems to be an emblem of royal rank. The Queen's crown, however, is of a distinctive flanged form (nos. 46 and 50).

The terracotta sculptures from Ife are far more numerous than the metal castings. They also show much more variation in style and in subject matter. There are a number of terracottas that were made as freestanding heads, not attached to any body

Figure 20 This pot, with the representation of a shrine bearing a naturalistic head flanked by two stylized heads, is evidence that these two styles were in contemporaneous use.

(nos. 47—49). The other Ife terracotta heads in this exhibition come from complete figures (nos. 50—54 and 59). The scale of representation varies from something very close to life size (no. 50) down to about 10 inches (no. 59). A number of Ife heads have what is known as a cat's whisker scarification found among several different peoples in Nigeria today (no. 51). It is particularly common nowadays among the Nupe, who claim that they copied it from the northern Yoruba. The fact that this type of scarification is represented several times in the art of Ife suggests that either it is an old and formerly widespread Yoruba mark or that these heads represent foreigners. Many of the Ife heads, in metal and in terracotta, bear fine lines engraved vertically down the face (nos. 42, 43, 45, 47, 48, 52—54, and 59). This seems to be a scarification that is no longer found among the Yoruba or their near neighbors.

There are also a number of pieces from Ife that are very highly stylized (no. 57). We know these are contemporary with the naturalistic heads, not simply an earlier and cruder form, nor a later more degenerate form, because a pot excavated at Obalara's Land, Ife, by Peter Garlake, has a naturalistic head flanked by two stylized heads, showing quite clearly that they were in contemporaneous use (fig. 20).

Although human beings are the most characteristic subject matter, animals are represented in Ife sculpture as well. Sculptures of sacrificial animals are found, mainly rams, and others which may be symbols of royal power like leopards. The two animal heads in this exhibition both come from the site of the grave of the Oni Lafogido and represent an elephant (no. 55) and probably a hippopotamus (no. 56). Both wear crowns and collars like those of the royal figures, so it may be supposed that these are royal beasts. It is interesting that the present Oni of Ife regards the elephant as his personal emblem and has a large collection of representations of elephants in the Palace.

The art of Ife seems to have both antecedents and descendents that we know something about, look-

Figure 21 This figure in terracotta from the Kubolaja shrine in Ife has a distribution of beads similar to those on several Nok works (nos. 9 and 12), and is related to Ife bronze works as well (nos. 44–46).

ing back to Nok and forward to Owo and Benin. The Nok and Ife artists are the only ones we know in the whole of Black Africa ever to attempt full-length sculpture in terracotta of human beings on a scale approaching life size (nos. 1 and 50). The distribution of beads on Nok figures can be closely paralleled in Ife works (nos. 9, 12, and fig. 21), while other works (nos. 44–46) show a general similarity. Another link can be seen in the stylistic convention by which the hem of the garment is represented (no. 44), which is identical with that on a figure from Kuchamfa, one of the Nok sites, and continues into the art of Owo (figs. 22–24). Another Nok link with Owo can be seen in the triangular treatment of toenails (no. 11 and fig. 25).

*Figures 22–24 The Nok fragment
(opposite page, bottom) uses the
same conventions to represent the hem
of the skirt and the fold at the waist
as are found later at Ife (this page, top,
left, and nos. 44 and 46) and Owo
(this page, bottom, left).*

*Figure 25 This foot from Owo exhibits
similar triangular toenails to those on
the Nok foot (no. 11).*

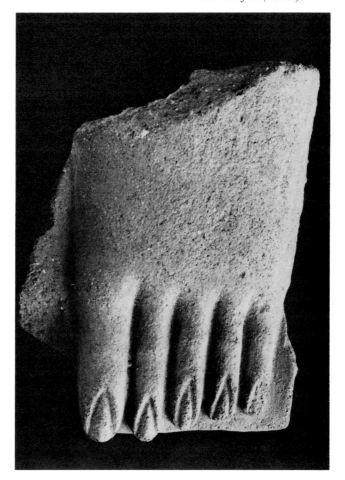

Figures 26 and 27 The protruding mouth on the head found at Tonga Nok (left, top) retains the blocked-out form one would expect to find in wood-carving rather than terracotta, and is strikingly similar to the mouth found on the piece from Yelwa (left, bottom).

Attention has already been drawn to some similarities of hairstyles between Nok and Ife (figs. 17 and 18). Some Ife heads also show a protruding mouth very similar to mouths on a Nok and a Yelwa piece (figs. 26–28), which seems to provide another link between Nok and Ife.

As more discoveries are made, more will be learned about the relationship between Nok and Ife. It may be that the link is less direct than I have implied, or that both derive from some as yet undiscovered ancestor, but it seems clear that there is a link of some sort between the two traditions. The forward links to Owo and Benin, only

Figure 28 This Ife head has a protruding mouth similar to that on the Nok and Yelwa pieces illustrated in figures 26 and 27.

touched on here, will be discussed in greater detail later in this essay.

Owo is another Yoruba city-state, like Ife. It lies roughly halfway between Ife and Benin, and its art shares in both traditions. All the sculptures from Owo in this exhibition come from excavations conducted by Dr. Eyo in 1971 on the site of Igbo'Laja. The material was probably deposited around the fifteenth century and includes a great variety of subjects.

Several of the Owo sculptures show characteristics of the Ife style. The striated heads (nos. 60, 61, and 64) show remarkable affinities to Ife heads (nos. 47, 48, and 52–54), although the clay from which they are made suggests that they were indeed made in Owo. The eyes are represented with an upper lid that overlaps the lower one at the corners; the upper lid itself is outlined with an incision just above its edge; the mouth often has a raised line around the edge, while the corners of the mouth are impressed. It should be noted, however, that unlike Ife heads, none of the Owo heads so far discovered wear crowns, but instead many wear simple caps (no. 63). In some cases, it is difficult to tell whether it is a cap or merely the hair that is represented (no. 65). Certain pieces also have particular features that can be seen on individual Ife works. For example, one man wears a beard that is represented by cross-hatched incised lines on a raised area (no. 63)—a convention one finds on a small head on top of a metal staff from Ife (fig. 29). The head also has furrowed brows that can be matched in a number of terracotta sculptures from Ife (fig. 30).

Figure 30 The furrowed brows on this head from Obalara's Land, Ife, are also similar to the brows on the Owo head with cross-hatched beard (no. 63).

Figure 29 This head on a bronze staff from Ita Yemoo, Ife, wears a beard represented by cross-hatched incised lines on a raised area like that seen on an Owo head (no. 63).

Figure 31 Characteristics of the post-Classical Ife style as seen on this head from the Mokuro Road, Ife, include bulging eyes, protruding lips, and stylized ears.

Figure 32 This Owo work (bottom), similar to the Ife head in figure 31, tends to suggest that Ife and Owo continued to have knowledge of one another for some time.

Although comparing the heads most clearly reveals the influences of Ife on Owo, there are similarities found on other kinds of sculptures as well. For example, like Ife artists (no. 58), those of Owo made pots with relief sculpture on them, though the degree of relief is different. One of these relief sculptures (no. 73) depicts a horned human face with snakes issuing from his nostrils, while on another (no. 74) a mudfish is swallowing a prawn, or a lobster. The motif of snakes issuing from the nostrils is widely spread across southwestern Nigeria and occurs on several Ife pieces as well as on the disc on the head of one of the Tsoede bronzes (no. 93).

We do not know a great deal yet about how the artistic traditions of the two city-states of Ife and Owo interrelated, but the art seems to have developed in a parallel manner in both centers. There is an Owo piece (fig. 32) that resembles the post-Classical Ife pieces (fig. 31), which was found with the main body of material with a single associated radiocarbon date of around the fifteenth century. If this single date can be relied on, the deposit would appear to date from the end of the Classical and beginning of the post-Classical period of Ife art.

This would tend to suggest that both areas continued for some time to produce art of high quality with knowledge of one another, and that the art was modified simultaneously in both centers in the direction of modern Yoruba style, with bulging eyes, protruding lips, and very stylized ears (no. 97).

Some Owo pieces show obvious links to Benin. Compare, for example, the four raised marks over each eyebrow on one fragment (no. 75) with the same scarification pattern seen on several Benin works (nos. 76–78). There are also a number of characteristics of subject matter both traditions share, including the mudfish (nos. 74 and 88) and the leopard (fig. 34 and nos. 81 and 82), though leopards are found also in Ife art. It is thought that

Owo craftsmen worked at times in Benin, as many sculptures in ivory and bronze found in Benin appear to be Owo works (no. 90).

While the Owo works serve to link Ife and Benin, there are certain characteristics that are unique to Owo art. The most striking of these is the great variety of sacrificial offerings depicted. For example, there are in this exhibition a female figure with a cock or chicken under her arm that is probably intended as a sacrifice (no. 66); an animal head and perhaps a mouse represented in the same way (nos. 67 and 68); and a cock or a chicken ready for sacrifice (no. 69). Owo art also represents some gruesome subjects that have not been found so far in other traditions. For example, a basket of severed heads (fig. 33) was found, as well as a

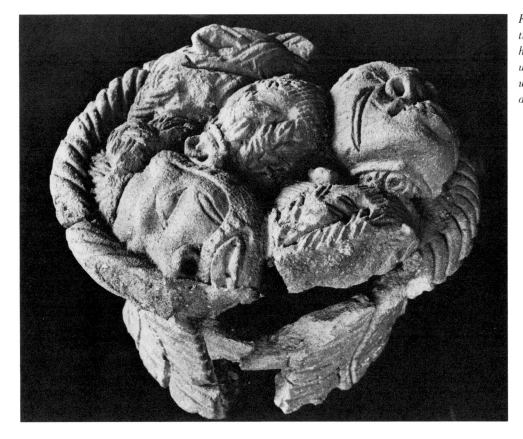

Figure 33 The representation of a basket of severed heads is an example of the use of gruesome subjects, which seems to be typical of ancient Owo art.

41

Figure 34 A leopard gnawing on a human leg is another example of the gruesome in Owo art.

sculpture of a leopard gnawing a human leg (fig. 34).

Ife political power began to wane in the sixteenth and seventeenth centuries, as the (Old) Oyo Kingdom began to dominate Yorubaland. At this time the Benin Empire was expanding. Thus, Ife influence on Owo undoubtedly lessened while that of Benin continued to grow. Today, the art of Owo still shows considerable influence from Benin, as do its political emblems and institutions.

BENIN presents us with the largest body of sculpture of all Nigeria's ancient traditions. Fortunately, in dealing with this art we are on somewhat surer grounds, for there are numerous oral traditions

and, from the late fifteenth century on, European documents from which to draw. There is also archaeological evidence which has so far thrown only a little light on how this art developed.

Dr. Eyo has summarized the traditions that show how the present dynasty in Benin came to be established from Ife. These same traditions record that when the Oba, or King, of the new dynasty died, his head was sent back to Ife for burial and in return a "bronze" head was sent from Ife to be placed on his ancestral shrine. After a time, usually calculated to be at the end of the fourteenth century, the King of Benin sent to Ife for a bronze-smith to teach his people how to make these commemorative heads for themselves. The man who was sent is said to have been named Igueghae. The traditions record that the kings of the earlier dynasty had already encouraged the crafts of wood carving and ivory carving, but not apparently bronze casting. The earliest Benin heads (nos. 76 and 77) are indeed very different from those of Ife; clearly, there was an already established art tradition whose conventions were carried over when the technique of casting was introduced. Excavations conducted by Graham Connah have shown that already in the thirteenth century the Bini were able to obtain bars of tin-bronze which they hammered into shape as bracelets and decorated by incision, but they were apparently not able to cast the metal themselves until the end of the fourteenth century. Only one casting, a small broken figure of an Oni of Ife, has been found in Benin to add concrete evidence to support the tradition that Ife castings used to be sent to Benin. However, the study of the zinc and lead contents of Ife and Benin works has allowed some sixty Benin pieces (almost all plaques of the Middle Period) to be identified as being composed, in part, of Ife metal, presumably obtained by melting down Ife castings when they had become old fashioned.

The art of Benin is clearly a royal art. Craftsmen were organized into guilds and they all lived together in the same quarter of the town. Apart from small items of accoutrement, like hip masks, which were part of the ceremonial dress of chiefs, no bronze casting could be commissioned by anyone except the King, unless he gave his permission. Another of the royal prerogatives was the right to half the ivory that any hunter obtained. One of each pair of tusks received the King's mark, and was assigned to him. Many of these he passed over to the ivory carvers.

William Fagg, the now-retired Keeper of the Department of Ethnography of the British Museum, divided Benin art into three periods. He began by defining the Middle Period as the time when the plaques were cast. Before this was the Early Period, and after it the Late Period. It is difficult to define the start and finish of the Middle Period, though there is a tradition which seems to suggest that the plaques began to be cast early in the sixteenth century. They are thought to have ceased being made at some uncertain date before 1700. This would mean that the Early Period runs from the introduction of bronze casting toward the end of the fourteenth century to the early sixteenth century; the Middle Period from the early sixteenth to the late seventeenth century; and the Late Period from the late seventeenth to 1897 when the

Oba of Benin was deposed by the British and casting ceased for a time.

Within these broad periods, a number of more precise dates have been established. In the early sixteenth century, the Oba Esigie introduced the title of Queen Mother, so the Queen Mother heads with the characteristic crown (no. 76) cannot be earlier than this date. (Of course, this ignores the possibility that the early heads with a rolled collar may also represent Queen Mothers.) The Oba Osemwede (1816–1848) introduced a crown with upswept projections that are to be seen on the latest heads and on the crowns still worn by the Oba of Benin (figs. 35 and 36). Heads that show this feature cannot antedate his reign.

The Early Period is represented in the exhibition by two works (nos. 76 and 77). These heads are very thin indeed, as can be seen from the dent in the forehead of one (no. 76) and the damage under the chin of the other (no. 77). Such bronze heads symbolized, rather than portrayed, the dead ruler and were cast during the installation of the new King.

An altar was set up in Benin in memory of Igueghae, the bronzesmith from Ife who introduced the art of casting to Benin. Upon it there were terracotta heads like one in this exhibition (no. 78), which clearly also copies the form of the Early Period heads (no. 77). We do know that the form of earlier heads was copied later in metal and it may be that later copies were made in terracotta of earlier forms of bronze heads. We, therefore, cannot be certain of the exact dates of some of these pieces, though it may be possible to establish them by thermoluminescence.

Another of the heads in the exhibition (no. 79) is a copy in a provincial style of the one mentioned above (no. 77). A head like this, together with

43

*Figure 35 This late Benin head shows
the upswept projections on the crown
that are still evident on the crown of
the Oba of Benin (fig. 36).*

*Figure 36 This photograph of a
former Oba of Benin, taken in 1959,
shows the projections on the crown
(fig. 35) and his ivory cuffs (no. 90).*

some figures, comes from the small town of Udo, some forty miles away from Benin. There are several of these heads in what we call the Udo style, and while we have no proof, it seems likely that these pieces were made there. Since they copy earlier period heads, they too have been thought to date from the Early Period; but thermoluminescence dates from two of these heads place them in the late sixteenth century — in other words, in the early part of the Middle Period.

At the end of the Early Period a number of very fine figures were cast, like the one thought to be a messenger (no. 80), probably carrying to Benin the emblems of authority sent from Ife when the new King of Benin acceded to the throne. The pair of leopards (nos. 81 and 82) are probably of this time as well. We have plaques in the Middle Period that show such leopards in position on shrines; so they existed in the Middle Period, if not sooner.

The Royal Palace in Benin, which covered about half of Benin City, had wooden columns supporting the roof. They were decorated with rectangular bronze plaques, many of which depicted scenes of life at court (nos. 83–87). The holes through which these plaques were nailed to the columns in the King's Palace can be seen on all examples in this exhibition. Usually two edges were folded around the rectangular timber. These plaques are provisionally dated from early in the sixteenth through the seventeenth century. Many show European traders in the costume of that period. According to a Benin tradition, after a group of Portuguese had assisted the people of Benin on an expedition against an enemy early in the sixteenth century, it was suggested that their success should be commemorated in the same way that Europeans commemorated such events. The rectangular form may be based on the shapes of pages in illustrated books, for this shape is not usually found in traditional African sculpture.

The plaques show an evolution in style from low to high relief. For example, one representing two men swinging on ropes (no. 84) is cast in relatively low relief, whereas another of a warrior chief with attendants (no. 86) is in very high relief, demonstrating the great technical skill with which projections from the background were handled by smiths in Benin. One or two plaques seem to make an attempt at Western perspective, presumably copying illustrations in books which gave rise to the form. The first one mentioned above (no. 84) has something of this quality about it, trying to indicate where the two figures swinging from ropes are to be found in space, whereas the other plaques (nos. 83 and 85–87) simply present the subject matter foursquare before us. The plaque of the warrior chief (no. 86) is a good example of what has been called social perspective, in that three supporting figures are shown at less than half the size of the three main figures, because they are less important socially. Notice also that in the background and even less conspicuous is the representation of a European. One wonders if this is a social comment. Many of the plaques represent animals: crocodiles (no. 87), fishes, leopards, and snakes, and a whole host of motifs from ceremonial swords to crescent moons.

Ivory was the second most important material in Benin art. Carvers made many items of ceremonial apparel for the King, like the cuff (no. 90), a tour de force that consists of two cylinders carved from a single piece of ivory. The inner cylinder can be moved independently of the outer one. This work was probably made by an Owo sculptor. The bowl (no. 91) was carved by a Benin sculptor and is one of the treasures removed from the King's own bedchamber by the British in 1897. Perhaps the best known type of ivory carving from Benin is the decorated entire tusk which, from the Middle Period on, was placed upon the heads cast for the ancestor shrine of the King. In the later period the heads became thicker and much heavier, sometimes weighing as much as 100 pounds; these served as very solid bases for heavy ivory tusks, which might be as much as 5 feet in length (fig. 37).

As the King of Benin was the principal patron of the craftsmen, it is perhaps surprising that the art survived his deposition in 1897 and subsequent exile. But when his successor came to the throne in 1914, he set about trying to restore some of the shrines (fig. 37); gradually over the years the skill of the Benin craftsmen has increased, largely under the patronage of the tourist trade. Nowadays, they are making figures in bronze that approach life size and half-figures that are fully of life size.

THE TSOEDE BRONZES(nos. 92–96 and figs. 13 and 14) are a group of works found in two villages, Jebba and Tada, in the area now occupied by the Nupe people. The traditional account of their origin has been recounted by Dr. Eyo. There has long been controversy about where these bronzes originated, but it has been generally agreed that they are unlikely to have been made in Igala as the Tsoede tradition would have us believe. Indeed, they seem to have been made in more than one center.

The seated figure from Tada (no. 92) appears to be the work of an Ife artist and may thus be considered the most ambitious work of Ife sculpture we know. Its complex asymmetrical posture is unique in African sculpture (though a fragmentary sculpture in terracotta in the Ife Museum might have

Figure 37 In the Middle and Late periods, the Benin memorial heads supported a carved ivory tusk (portions of two of these are visible in this picture). This photograph shows one of the shrines set up after the restoration of the throne in 1914.

been in a similar pose). Most African sculptures are symmetrically balanced about a vertical axis, whereas this one is seated with the left knee lying on the ground and the right knee raised. The arms are broken, but these, too, were in an asymmetrical pose. The figure is also unusual in that the proportions of the head and limbs correspond to those of a real human being. In other figures from Ife the head is about a quarter of the overall height, while the legs are greatly reduced in proportion to real people. This piece, although clearly in Ife style, may have been made elsewhere, but until more evidence comes to light, it must remain one of the most intriguing works in the whole corpus of African art.

The figures of a warrior and a bowman (nos. 93 and 94) are in a completely different style but are clearly related to each other, while the facial features on the figure with a staff (no. 95) are similarly treated — the round bulging eye outlined by a raised line and the kidney-shaped mouth with parted lips. The missing female figure from Jebba (fig. 14) also shows these same stylistic features. The figure with hands clasped (no. 96) is a little different, and distinctly Yoruba in style. Recent studies comparing the details of the warrior and bowman (nos. 93 and 94) with Owo works in bronze and ivory have led to the suggestion that they may be the work of Owo craftsmen. If they are, then the figure with a staff (no. 95) should be similarly attributed. Moreover, in view of the similarity of the Owo and Ife terracottas, if the seated figure (no. 92) was not made at Ife, we have to consider the possibility that it too may have been made in Owo.

There are links between some of these pieces and other traditions. The face on the disc of the headdress worn by the warrior (no. 93), with the snakes emerging from the nostrils and horns on his head, is found in both Ife and Owo art (no. 73), and in

works found in Benin but made by foreign artists. This face also has Benin scarification over its eyes. If these pieces were indeed made in Owo, they are Yoruba work, since Owo is a Yoruba town. However, they are sufficiently distinctive to merit an independent naming. The figure with hands clasped (no. 96) cannot be assigned to a specific place of origin, though there can be little doubt that it is a Yoruba work. The large bulging eyes, the highly stylized ears, and the protruding lips all distinguish what I have called the post-Classical style, which seems to lead into the modern Yoruba style. The gesture made by the hands, one of which is grasping the thumb of the other, is characteristic of the Ogboni Society, which is responsible for the cult of the earth in Yorubaland (no. 97). Thus, it would appear that all these pieces grouped together as the Tsoede bronzes come from Yorubaland, but they may come from three different centers: Ife (no. 92), Owo (nos. 93–95), and a place as yet unidentified (no. 96). Only two of them have been dated: the Tada seated figure (no. 92) to the late thirteenth/early fourteenth century, and the figure of a warrior (no. 93) to the fourteenth century.

OTHER WORKS in the exhibition give no more than a token representation of other art traditions from Nigeria. One (no. 97) is from a group of Yoruba metal castings that probably date from the eighteenth century. This piece comes from Iperu and is usually said to represent Onile, the spirit of the earth (literally "the owner of the earth") who is the center of the cult of the Ogboni Society. Another figure from this group is still in use in an Ogboni house in Ede, whither it is said to have been taken from the town of Owu, in Yorubaland. Nowadays, the Ogboni Society is the main patron of the traditional bronze casters in Yorubaland and the very protrusive eyes shaped like half an almond seem to be characteristic of bronze castings made for this Society. One scholar has identified this particular work as representing Ajagbo, a terrible Alafin (King) of Oyo, who was deified as a vengeful spirit whose image is used in the detection and punishment of those who betrayed the secrets of the Ogboni Society. Ajagbo, however, is closely related to the spirit of the earth, and it would seem strange that a male ruler should be represented by a female effigy. In any case, the bulging eyes, flat protruding lips, and stylized ears are features of modern Yoruba sculpture that also characterize the post-Classical Ife style (fig. 31). Since such features were already established on this eighteenth-century piece, it seems to support the dating of the post-Classical Ife works to the late fifteenth to seventeenth centuries.

The soapstone sculptures of Esie (nos. 98 and 99) are an enigma. The only hint of their date comes from a thermoluminescence date of about A.D. 1100 for a fragment of terracotta sculpture found with them. It is by no means certain that the stone sculptures are of the same age. These two pieces are taken from a group of some eight hundred sculptures found lying in the bush near the Yoruba village of Esie (fig. 15). It is not at all sure where the Esie sculptures were carved, but some of the traditions in Esie certainly suggest that they were brought there from elsewhere.

These sculptures represent men and women whose very elaborate hairstyles are rendered with great accuracy in soft stone. Many of them, of both sexes, carry weapons, and most are represented as sitting on stools, wearing simple necklaces and bracelets. Some play musical instruments. Sometimes, though not in the two pieces shown here, the feet are represented simply by incision on the base of the stool. The scarification pattern on one (no. 98) resembles that on Igbo-Ukwu sculptures (nos. 31 and 36), but there is no other evidence of any connection between these two centers.

The Ikom monoliths from the Cross River area, known as *akwanshi* (no. 100 and fig. 16), have been dated by Philip Allison on grounds of oral tradition to span the period from the sixteenth to the early twentieth centuries. These stone sculptures lie on land occupied by five subgroups of the Ekoi or Ejagham people. At the time of the British occupation, the menfolk were fierce headhunters. Like the Igbo, their society was stateless, but small groups recognized the religious and ceremonial authority of the *Ntoon*. The stone figures occur only in a very small area and, according to local informants, represent ancestors. The *Nta* subgroup claim that their *akwanshi* represent *Ntoons*, who were buried among the *akwanshi*, and Philip Allison reports that imported brass rods and crockery can be seen protruding from the surface in several places. They listed forty *Ntoons* who probably reigned for about ten years each, since they were old when they reached the title.

There is some variation in style between the sites, but all are characterized by the carving with a minimum of effort of natural boulders into the representation of human beings, usually with a very prominent navel, but with all the other features represented in a fairly low relief, by pecking away the surface of the rock. It is to be hoped that these interesting sites can be excavated and dated before they disappear, for already the smugglers have been attacking them with tow trucks.

Whether or not we know very much about the cultural background of these artistic traditions, the great antiquity of some of them and the great variety of their sculptural forms and media are impressive enough. Over the last decade we have learned a great deal more and we can expect each decade for centuries to come to yield even further evidence, allowing us to fill the gaps in time and space and thus eventually to write a coherent history of Nigerian sculpture.

NOK

1 HEAD

c. 500 B.C./c. A.D. 200
Terracotta; h. 36 cm. (14³/16 in.)
From Rafin Kura, Nok
National Museum, Lagos, 79.R.1

The Nok terracottas are the earliest known sculptures from ancient Nigeria, dating at least from the middle of the first millennium B.C. This head, the largest so far published from Nok, is almost lifesize and was part of a full-length figure. The piercing of the eyes, nostrils, mouth, and ears is typical of Nok sculpture. Another distinguishing feature is the triangular form of the eyes, with the eyebrow balancing the sweep of the lower lid. The elaborate hairstyle here includes several buns with holes, which may have been for feathers, and three strings of beads, plaited fiber, or possibly iron chain, running across the top of the forehead.

2 HEAD

c. 500 B.C./c. A.D. 200
Terracotta; h. 22.9 cm. (9 in.)
From Nok
National Museum, Jos, 62.J.24

This bearded and moustached man wears a headband and tresses down each cheek and on the back of the neck. Above the headband his hair is represented by rings in relief. The balanced forms of eyebrow and lower lid here form a circular pattern, as is frequently the case on Nok heads. The small projecting beard is also characteristic.

3 HEAD

c. 500 B.C./c. A.D. 200
Terracotta; h. 14 cm. (5½ in.)
From Rafin Maigaskiya, Nok
National Museum, Jos, 64.J.58

This head, too, features a beard that projects from the bottom of the chin and a caplike coiffure, with tresses hanging down the sides for the full length of the face. It appears that the figure also wore a moustache in the form of small tufts on each side of the mouth (*opposite*).

5 HEAD

c. late 4th century B.C.
Terracotta; h. 26 cm. (10^{1}/4 in.)
From Jemaa-Kafanchan Road
National Museum, Lagos, 63.J.236

This elegant, cylindrical head has been dated by thermoluminescence to around the late fourth century B.C. On the top of the head is part of the left hand holding an object. The back of this sculpture is unfinished, indicating it was probably affixed to a building or shrine (*opposite*).

4 HEAD

c. 500 B.C./c. A.D. 200
Terracotta; h. 10 cm. (3^{15}/16 in.)
From Jemaa
National Museum, Jos, 58.22

This head shows the spherical shape, one of the three basic geometric forms in which the Nok artists conceived the human head, the others being the cylinder and the cone. He wears a full moustache and a beard, most of which has broken off. A single ridge of hair runs across the top of his head, while the rest of the head is closely shaven from ear to ear. The area between the left eyebrow and the left eye is rouletted in the same way as the hair; this is the only Nok head with this feature. The peculiar angle and elongation of the ears can be found on many Nok heads.

6 THE JEMAA HEAD
c. 5th century B.C.
Terracotta; h. 25 cm. (9¹³/₁₆ in.)
From Tsauni Camp, Jemaa
National Museum, Lagos, 79.R.2

Perhaps the best known of all Nok terracottas, the Jemaa Head, found in 1943, was one of the two heads that convinced Bernard Fagg there was an unknown culture of considerable antiquity in the area around Nok. The relatively simple features delineated on the smooth surface of the head — with the flaring upper lips of the large mouth almost touching the nostrils — give this head tremendous power. The hairstyle consists of a band of dressed hair reaching from ear to ear, with three horizontal tiers arranged behind. A thermoluminescence date of c. 510 ± 230 has been obtained for this head (*opposite*).

7 HEAD
c. 500 B.C./c. A.D. 200
Terracotta; h. 19 cm. (7¹/₂ in.)
From Jemaa
National Museum, Lagos, 47.2

This head shows the conical form. The hair is represented as a ring of buns around the head, with two extra buns at the temples and a peak at the center. Nowadays, hairstyles in Africa may reflect merely changing fashions, though many traditional styles are restricted to members of particular cults. Either of these may have been the case at Nok.

8 HEAD WITH INFLATED CHEEKS

c. 500 B.C./c. A.D. 200
Terracotta; h. 9.2 cm. (3⅝ in.)
From Jemaa
National Museum, Jos, 48.J.5

This unusual head, its cheeks puffed up
and lips pushed forward, possibly represents a musician playing a reeded instrument, though no trace of an instrument can
be seen. The hairstyle includes a raised
band stretching from ear to ear, a flat bun
at the center back surrounded by several
semicircular flat bands, and two rows of
indented circles just above the neck.
Heavy beetling brows overhang the deep-
set eyes.

9 KNEELING MAN

c. 500 B.C./c. A.D. 200
Terracotta; h. 10.6 cm. (4³⁄₁₆ in.)
From Bwari, near Abuja
National Museum Lagos, 60.J.2

Though small in size, this beautifully
detailed figure well illustrates the importance of jewelry in the Nok culture. The
kneeling man seems literally weighed down
by his bracelets, anklets, the thick girdle
around his waist, the heavy collar round
his neck, and the elaborate strings of beads
draped over his chest and back. The hairstyle includes six buns and tresses down
the neck. Holes beside the head and waist
on opposite sides suggest that the figure
may have been used as a pendant (*opposite
page*).

10 WOMAN WEARING A HOOD

c. mid-5th century B.C.
Terracotta; h. 31.5 cm. (12³/₈ in.)
Provenance uncertain
National Museum, Lagos (Jos N. 1018.1)

Another full-length figure, like
number 9, this one of a woman is
mounted on a base featuring a
Janus-like composition of two
faces, a motif found on other Nok
pieces. This example has a very
Yoruba-looking face, and the
whole piece bears a general
resemblance to an *epa* mask used
by the Yoruba of Ekiti at the
present time. A small child was
held by the woman, whose hands
and forearms are now missing,
between her breasts and at her
waist. A hood, probably of animal
skin, covers her head, falls down
her back, and is surmounted by a
small cap. This piece has been
dated by thermoluminescence to
about the mid-fifth century B.C.

11 FOOT

c. 500 B.C./c. A.D. 200
Terracotta; h. 15 cm. (5¹⁵/₁₆ in.)
From the Big Paddock, Nok
National Museum, Jos, 148

This fragment of a left foot and
part of a lower leg, found at the
site shown in figure 1, is from a
large figure. The highly developed decorative sense of the Nok
sculptors is indicated by the treatment of the anklets and the decoration of the bottom edge, which
echoes the triangular form of the
toenails. Triangular toenails are a
regular feature of Nok sculpture,
as they also are in the later sculpture of Owo (fig. 25).

c. 500 B.C./c. A.D. 200
Terracotta; h. 14 cm. (5½ in.)
From Kutofo
National Museum, Lagos, 60.J.18.1

This fragment may have been
broken from a pot or it may have
been a decorative element on a
larger figure. The work exhibits
typical Nok characteristics:
pierced eyes, nostrils, and ears;
profuse beadwork, including
armlets, anklets, and necklaces;
and an elaborate hairstyle with
the hair dressed in rings on the
crown of the head and tresses at
the sides. The pointed beard also
is typical. The necklaces are worn
here in the same arrangement as
they are on number 9, and can be
compared to how jewelry is worn
on some Ife terracotta and bronze
figures (fig. 21 and nos. 44 and 45).

13 ELEPHANT HEAD

c. 500 B.C./c. A.D. 200
Terracotta; h. 19 cm. (7½ in.)
From Agwazo Mine, Udegi,
near Nassarawa
National Museum, Jos, N291.1

This elephant head — with its
large ears, striated trunk, and
characteristic stylized Nok eyes
— is articulated at the neck in
such a way as to suggest that it was
attached to an upright spine,
which might indicate that the animal was sitting on his haunches
(*opposite*).

14 SEATED MAN

c. 200/c. 700
Terracotta; h. 20.5 cm. (8 in.)
From Yelwa Mound, R.S. 63/32
National Museum, Kaduna

This seated figure from Yelwa — with
its pierced eyes, nostrils, and mouth, its
moustache tufts and projecting beard, its
asymmetrical pose, and its simplified
bracelets and necklaces — seems to show a
decline of the Nok style-tradition (figs. 26
and 27).

IGBO-UKWU

15 BOWL ON A STAND

9th/10th century
Leaded bronze; h. 20.3 cm. (8 in.)
Presumed from Igbo Isaiah, Igbo-Ukwu
National Museum, Lagos, 39.1.1

Digging for a water cistern at Igbo-Ukwu in 1938 disturbed a deposit of bronze castings from a storehouse of ritual objects (fig. 4), including this shallow, widely flared bowl sitting on a hollow barrel-shaped base. The decorative motifs of the bowl are repeated in the stand: a band of hatched triangles and a band with representations of insects (mantises, beetles, and crickets) and openwork spirals. The widest band in the center of the stand is decorated with a dense pattern of lozenges with circles on a granulated ground. The vessel was made in two parts and fitted together by casting on the middle band of insects and spirals.

16 ROPED POT ON A STAND

9th/10th century
Leaded bronze; h. 32.3 cm. (12^{11}/$_{16}$ in.)
From Igbo Isaiah, Igbo-Ukwu
National Museum, Lagos, 79.R.4

This elegant vessel was excavated in the remains of a ritual store-house. It is technically the most elaborate casting from Igbo-Ukwu. It consists of an elongated globular waterpot cast upon an openwork stand, both enclosed by a ropework with reef knots at the junctions. The provision of the stand in both this and number 15 perhaps reflects the tradition still maintained in this part of Nigeria that sacred water should not touch the earth before it is used in ritual ceremonies.

17 BOWL

9th/10th century
Leaded bronze; d. 41.9 cm. (16^{5}/$_{16}$ in.)
Presumed from Igbo Isaiah, Igbo-Ukwu
National Museum, Lagos, 39.1.2

Calabashes, or gourds, cut in various ways are used throughout Nigeria as drinking vessels (fig. 19). They often have decorative designs cut into the surface and on very rare occasions are decorated with metal attachments. This finely cast bowl unfortunately has a large piece broken out of one side where the casting is very thin. That its use was ritual rather than functional is indicated by its single handle, despite its large size, and the detailed surface decoration, here composed of rows of tiny spirals and of square relief dots (*opposite*).

18 BOWL

9th/10th century
Leaded bronze; d. 25.7 cm. (10 in.)
From Igbo Isaiah, Igbo-Ukwu
National Museum, Lagos, 79.R.3 (39.1.4)

This large bowl appears to be based on half of a large globular calabash,
decorated outside with four bands of raised horizontal and vertical loops.
The interior of this and similar bowls from Igbo-Ukwu is unadorned.

19 BOWL

9th/10th century
Leaded bronze; d. 26.4 cm. (10⁵/16 in.)
Presumed from Igbo Isaiah, Igbo-Ukwu
National Museum, Lagos, 54.4.22

This was one of the original Igbo-Ukwu bronzes dug up in 1938. The discoverer,
Isaiah Anozie, used the bowl to water his goats until 1954, when it was acquired by
Kenneth Murray, head of the Federal Department of Antiquities. Its decoration —
bands of quatrefoil, lozenges, bosses, and stringwork, alternating with unadorned
bands — is typical of Igbo-Ukwu ornament.

20 CRESCENTIC BOWL
9th/10th century
Leaded bronze; l. 13.9 cm. (5⁷/16 in.)
From Igbo Isaiah, Igbo-Ukwu
National Museum, Lagos, 39.1.8

This small bowl is based on the crescent shape of a small flat calabash cut through
in the vertical plane in contrast to numbers 17—19, which are cut horizontally. As on
many of these ritual vessels, there are three conical bosses on either side of the
handle. It may have been a drinking cup.

21 CRESCENTIC BOWL

9th/10th century
Leaded bronze; l. 17.8 cm. (7 in.)
Presumed from Igbo Isaiah, Igbo-Ukwu
National Museum, Lagos, 39.1.5

The decoration of this small crescentic bowl is similar to but not identical
with number 20. It, too, may have been a drinking cup.

22 VESSEL IN THE FORM OF A SHELL

9th/10th century
Leaded bronze; l. 30.5 cm. (12 in.)
Presumed from Igbo Isaiah, Igbo-Ukwu
National Museum, Lagos, 39.1.12

This beautifully conceived small ceremonial vessel is in the form of a
shell, probably a Triton. Scattered over the delicate network of raised and
incised patterns that connect each of the vessel's whorls are crickets and
flies. The pointed end is animated by a group of four frogs, whose heads
are inside the mouths of snakes that spring from raised rings.

23 VESSEL IN THE FORM OF A SHELL SURMOUNTED BY AN ANIMAL

9th/10th century
Leaded bronze; l. 20.6 cm. (8¹/₈ in.)
Presumed from Igbo Isaiah, Igbo-Ukwu
National Museum, Lagos, 39.1.13

A complicated, well-executed casting, this vessel, with its jewel-like decorations, is in the shape of a shell. It differs from other vessels of the type
found at the same site in its smaller size, in the form of the bands of decoration, and in the inclusion of a curious long-tailed animal, probably a
leopard, standing on a circular pedestal.

24 PEAR-SHAPED BOWL

9th/10th century
Leaded bronze; l. 10.2 cm. (4 in.)
Presumed from Igbo Isaiah, Igbo-Ukwu
National Museum, Lagos, 39.1.11

This small pear-shaped bowl has a pouring lip, which suggests that it was
a dipper. The raised decorations are spirals with dots in the centers and
circles strung through the middle with dots, all alternating with bands of
dots. A small conical boss is placed on either side of the handle.

25 ORNATE STAFF HEAD

9th/10th century
Leaded bronze; h. 14.5 cm. (5^{11}/$_{16}$ in.)
From Igbo Isaiah, Igbo-Ukwu
National Museum, Lagos, Is348

The decoration of this staff head — one of a
number found at Igbo-Ukwu — is devoid of
the beads found on other similar ornaments
and is concentrated into horizontal bands
that include the representations of flies,
frogs, beetles, and snakes. From the center
of the disc-shaped top emerge three rings
decorated with triple strings. The work
retains the stump of an iron blade by which
it was attached to the staff.

26 ORNATE STAFF HEAD

9th/10th century
Leaded bronze; h. 17.5 cm. (6⁷/8 in.)
Presumed from Igbo Isaiah, Igbo-Ukwu
National Museum, Lagos, 39.1.30

Originally, this staff head would
have been encrusted with beads
of different colors strung through
loops on the casting to form lines
that emphasized the complex decorative scheme. The most conspicuous sculptural detail of the
design is four whorls in the form
of snakes that look alternately
upward and downward. The strap
on top lacks its middle portion.

27 CYLINDRICAL STAFF ORNAMENT

9th/10th century
Leaded bronze; h. 14.5 cm.
(5¹¹/16 in.)
Presumed from Igbo Isaiah, Igbo-Ukwu
National Museum, Lagos, 39.1.18

Finely detailed birds, small granulated bosses, and variously col-
ored beads decorate this large
cylindrical ornament designed for
the middle of a staff. Over sixty
thousand beads were found in the
excavations at Igbo Isaiah
(*opposite*).

28 CYLINDRICAL STAFF
ORNAMENT
9th/10th century
Leaded bronze; h. 16.3 cm. (6⁷/16 in.)
Presumed from Igbo Isaiah, Igbo-Ukwu
National Museum, Lagos, 39.1.16

This ingenious hollow ornament
in the shape of a densely pat-
terned and textured coil was probably used to decorate a ceremonial staff. At each end is a coiled
snake with an egg in its mouth.

29 SPIRAL SNAKE ORNAMENT

9th/10th century
Copper; h. 16.3 cm. (6⁷/₁₆ in.)
From Igbo Isaiah, Igbo-Ukwu
National Museum, Lagos, Is249

This coiled snake is made of copper and, like the snakes'
heads of number 28, holds an egg in its mouth. It was probably set into the end of a staff with the snake's head and neck
lying on the surface of the staff. It may have been on a staff by
itself, or put at the opposite end to a larger staff ornament like
those in numbers 25 and 26.

30 SPIRAL SNAKE ORNAMENT

9th/10th century
Copper; h. 16.1 cm. (6⁵/₁₆ in.)
Presumed from Igbo Isaiah, Igbo-Ukwu
National Museum, Lagos, 39.1.27

Both this and number 29 consist of coiled twists of copper
wire that were probably not cast but rather made by twisting,
smithing, and chasing techniques. This snake, unlike those
of numbers 28 and 29, does not hold an egg in its mouth.

31 PENDANT REPRESENTING A HUMAN HEAD

9th/10th century
Leaded bronze; h. 7.6 cm. (3 in.)
Presumed from Igbo Isaiah, Igbo-Ukwu
National Museum, Lagos, 39.1.19

One of the few human representations found at Igbo-Ukwu, this small head is in the same class of objects as the double egg and animal head pendants (nos. 32–34). Raised scarification marks follow a pattern that can also be seen on the rider of number 36 (*opposite*).

32 DOUBLE EGG PENDANT

9th/10th century
Leaded bronze; h. 21.6 cm. overall (8½ in.)
From Igbo Isaiah, Igbo-Ukwu
National Museum, Lagos, 79.R.5 (Is367)

This unusual pendant portrays a bird lying on top of a pair of large eggs. The eggs, connected by an ornamental arch, each bear representations of three flies. The bird faces protectively downward, with its wings curving widely away from the body and then turning back under the tail. Its watchful eyes are particularly prominent. Along the back of each egg runs a row of loops to which wire chains with beads and bells are attached.

9th/10th century
Leaded bronze; h. 8.6 cm. (3³/₈ in.)
Presumed from Igbo Isaiah, Igbo-Ukwu
National Museum, Lagos, 39.1.21

This pendant, representing a ram's head, is
characteristically ornate. Running down
the center of the face are four ovals defined
by raised dots and vertical lines. To either
side, above the mouth and nostrils, is the
representation of a fly. The horns curve
around to enclose both ears and eyes. The
head is surmounted by a double-ended
trumpet-shaped decoration.

34 PENDANT REPRESENTING AN ELEPHANT'S HEAD

9th/10th century
Leaded bronze; h. 7.4 cm. (2 15/16 in.)
Presumed from Igbo Isaiah, Igbo-Ukwu
National Museum, Lagos, 39.1.20

This pendant in the shape of an elephant's head carries a lozenge pattern of decoration made with lines of raised dots. The trunk and tusks are curved sharply under. Comparison of this work with the elephant head from Nok (no. 13) clearly demonstrates the Igbo-Ukwu artists' highly evolved decorative and schematic approach to the representation of natural forms.

35 SCABBARD

9th/10th century
Leaded bronze; h. 42.9 cm. (16⅞ in.)
Presumed from Igbo Isaiah, Igbo-Ukwu
National Museum, Lagos, 39.1.32

Along the whole length of this sword scabbard runs the body of a snake
with a head at each end. In the snake's mouth at the flange end is the head
of a frog; at the other end the snake holds the snout of a pangolin, which
forms the decorative loop at the end of the scabbard. This piece demonstrates how well the artists of Igbo-Ukwu could integrate decorative motifs
and formal design.

36 FLY WHISK HANDLE

9th/10th century
Leaded bronze; h. 15.7 cm. (6³/₁₆ in.)
From Igbo Richard, Igbo-Ukwu
National Museum, Lagos, IR359

This bronze ornament, excavated from a
burial chamber (fig. 5), was most likely the
handle of a fly whisk. The horse and rider
are not naturalistically rendered, but are
executed with the same attention to decorative detail that is found on all Igbo-Ukwu
works. This is demonstrated in the costume
and accoutrements of the rider — his headdress, belt, pouch, and the fly whisk he
holds in his right hand — as well as in the
overall varied patterning of the horse and
the handle itself.

37 PENDENT MEDALLION

9th/10th century
Leaded bronze; h. 6.4 cm. (2½ in.)
Presumed from Igbo Isaiah, Igbo-Ukwu
National Museum, Lagos, 39.1.24

Snakes once again dominate as a decorative motif in this small but complex medallion. Out of the middle of a figure eight issue four snakes that curve around to echo the figure eight and terminate in heads, each of which holds an egg. A cricket or grasshopper sits atop the central knot of the motif.

38 POTSTAND

9th/10th century
Leaded bronze; diam. 16.8 cm. (6⅝ in.)
Presumed from Igbo Isaiah, Igbo-Ukwu
National Museum, Lagos, 39.1.14

This stand for a round-bottomed pot (compare nos. 15 and 16) demonstrates again the elegant design sense and attraction to geometric patterning of the artists of Igbo-Ukwu. Covering the top and external portions of this hollow ring is an elaborate design of seemingly equilateral triangles connected by dots and filled in by three or four lines of small dots running in alternate directions.

IFE

12th/15th century
Zinc brass; h. 31 cm. (12³/16 in.)
From Wunmonije Compound, Ife
Museum of Ife Antiquities, 11

The Yoruba city-state of Ife, according to oral tradition, was the place where the gods descended to create the world. The art of Ife is unique in Africa for its naturalistic treatment of the human form. This lifesize head represents a dead King, or Oni, in his prime. Moustache and beard of real hair might have been attached to the holes around the mouth and chin. All the Oni heads exhibit a serenity and dignity appropriate to the qualities of kingship these heads embody.

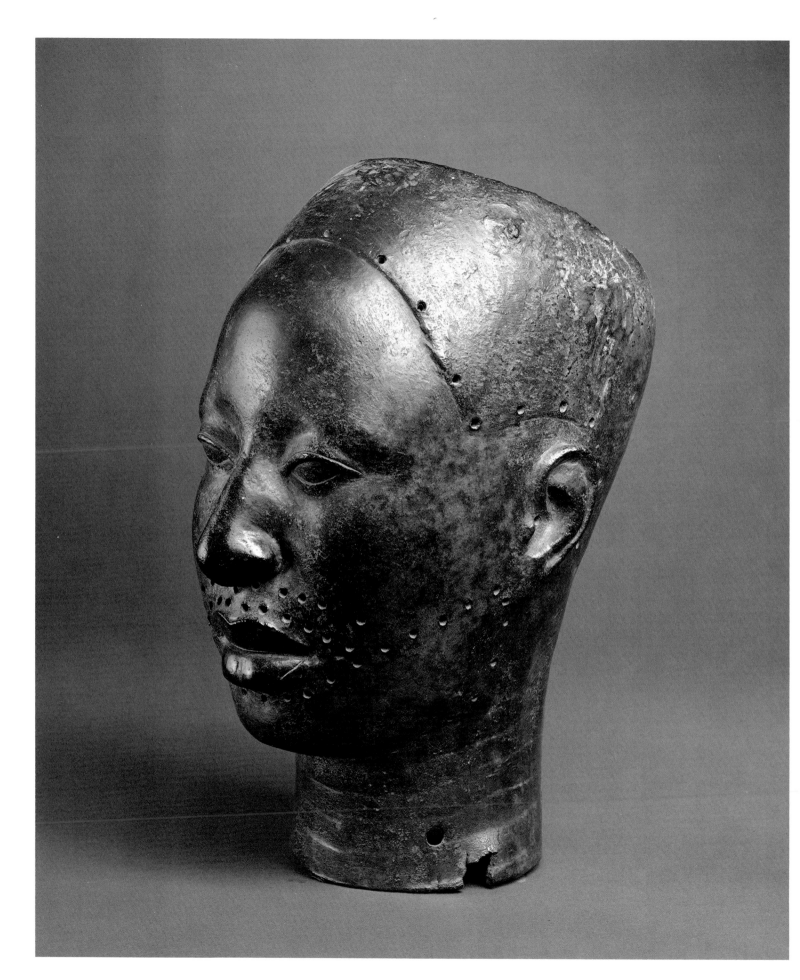

40 HEAD OF AN ONI

12th/15th century
Zinc brass; h. 29.5 cm.(11⁵/8 in.)
From Wunmonije Compound, Ife
Museum of Ife Antiquities, 12

These heads were used in second
burial ceremonies some time after
the funeral of the King. The head
carried the crown of the dead
King and was attached to a
wooden body by the holes in its
neck. The ritual demonstrated
that, although the King was dead,
the power of the office continued.
After use they were brought to a
shrine in the Palace. The Palace
was reduced in size early in the
nineteenth century and a compound named after the Oni Wunmonije was built over the site
(*opposite*).

41 MASK SAID TO REPRESENT
THE ONI OBALUFON

12th/15th century
Copper; h. 29.5 cm. (11⁵/8 in.)
From the Oni's Palace, Ife
Museum of Ife Antiquities, 17

Despite its weight (12³/4 lbs.),
this mask with slits under the
eyes was clearly intended to be
worn. It is a remarkable work
made entirely of copper, a particularly difficult material to cast
when not alloyed with other
metal. The perfection of this casting was probably achieved by
attaching the mold to the crucible
holding the metal so as to exclude
as much air as possible while the
metal was being poured. By tradition, this mask is said to represent the Oni Obalufon, who is
credited with having introduced
the art of bronze casting into Ife.

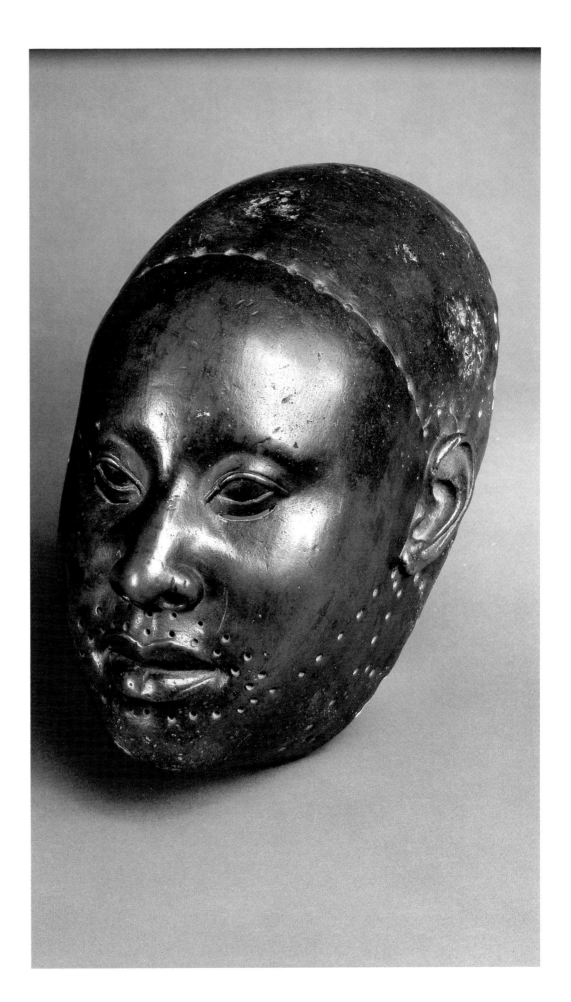

42 CROWNED HEAD OF AN ONI

12th/15th century
Zinc brass; h. 24 cm. (9⁷/16 in.)
From Wunmonije Compound, Ife
Museum of Ife Antiquities, 19 (79.R.11)

The features on this smaller-than-lifesize
crowned head are particularly delicate,
leading some to hypothesize this head may
portray a female Oni. The refined overall
patterns, which probably represent a scarification, also serve to emphasize the delicate modeling of the features. The projec-
tion on the crown is broken (*opposite*).

43 HEAD OF AN ONI

12th/15th century
Copper; h. 29 cm. (11⁷/16 in.)
From Wunmonije Compound, Ife
Museum of Ife Antiquities, 6

Several of the lifesize heads found at Wunmonije Compound in 1939 bear traces of
paint — white in the corners of the eyes,
black on the pupils, and red on the
neck. This one also bears lines of red and
black paint above and below the eyes.

44 FIGURE OF AN ONI

Early 14th/early 15th century
Zinc brass; h. 47.1 cm. (18⁹/16 in.)
From Ita Yemoo, Ife
Museum of Ife Antiquities, 79.R.12

This statue of an Oni, dated by thermoluminescence, is the only unbroken full-
length "bronze" standing figure discovered
in Ife to date. He wears the traditional
regalia: a crown, a heavy beaded collar
around the neck, a heavy rope of beads
around the outer edge of the trunk, finer
necklaces covering the chest with a double
bow in the center — a badge of his office as
King. In his left hand he holds a ram's horn
filled with magical substances (called
ashe) and in his right a sceptre made of
beads and cloth, both symbols of his
authority and power. The head is about a
quarter of the overall height of the figure, a
proportion characteristic especially of West
African sculpture.

45 UPPER HALF OF A FIGURE OF AN ONI

Late 15th/early 16th century
Zinc brass; h. 37 cm. (14⁹/16 in.)
From Wunmonije Compound, Ife
Museum of Ife Antiquities, 13 (79.R.9)

This top of a figure, although similar to number 44, appears to be the work of a different artist, and its thermoluminescence date shows it to be probably a century younger. Two heads from the find (which included nos. 39, 40, 42, and 43) have produced thermoluminescence dates between the late fourteenth and mid-sixteenth centuries (*opposite*).

46 CEREMONIAL VESSEL WITH FIGURE OF A QUEEN

12th/15th century
Zinc brass; h. 12.4 cm. (4⁷/8 in.)
From Ita Yemoo, Ife
National Museum, Lagos, L92.58

Around the bowl of this small vessel is wound the figure of a Queen. She wears a four-tiered crown with a crest and holds in her right hand a sceptre decorated with a human head. The bowl is placed on top of a stool with circular seat and base and a looped handle, which in turn is supported by a four-legged stool.
The rather corroded state of this piece somewhat spoils the detail the artist achieved in very small scale.

47 HEAD
12th/15th century
Terracotta; h. 25 cm. (9¹³/₁₆ in.)
From the Iwinrin Grove, Ife
National Museum, Lagos, 79.R.14 (Ife 22)

This head comes from a grove on the edge of Ife that originally housed a large number of terracotta sculptures, several of them full-length figures of life size. This head does not come
from a figure but was made to be freestanding. It wears a cap similar to those worn in numbers 48 and 49. In addition, a circlet is worn round the head, with three bell-like ornaments
(one now broken away) projecting forward over the brow (*opposite*).

48 HEAD
12th/15th century
Terracotta; h. 30.2 cm. (11⁷/₈ in.)
From Odo Ogbe Street, Ife
National Museum, Lagos, 73.2.71

This lifesize freestanding head with facial
scarification exhibits the cool, detached
expression typical of Ife representations
of the human face. The delicate modeling
is typical of the highest quality of Ife
sculpture.

12th/15th century
Terracotta; h. 32.8 cm. (12^{15}/16 in.)
From the Oni's Palace, Ife
Museum of Ife Antiquities, 20 (79.R.10)

Terracotta sculptures from Ife are far more numerous than metal castings and show more variation in style and subject matter. This fine freestanding head shows particular attention to the details of hair texture and cap. It is said always to have been kept in the Royal Palace and to represent the usurper Lajuwa, who seized the throne when Oni Aworokolokin died. It resembles very closely the heads from Wunmonije Compound (nos. 39, 40, 42, and 43), and demonstrates the typical Ife style-characteristics: overhanging of the corners of the lower lid by the upper; the incised line parallel to the edge of the upper lid; the raised edge of the lips; the impressed corners of the mouth; and the grooves around the neck (*opposite*).

50 HEAD OF A QUEEN
12th/13th century
Terracotta; h. 25 cm. (9^{13}/16 in.)
From Ita Yemoo, Ife
Museum of Ife Antiquities, 79.R.7

This head, originally from a full-length figure, is the most elaborate terracotta head found so far in Ife. The complex five-tiered, beaded crown indicates that it represents a Queen. Traces of red and white paint survive on the crown, and there is red paint on the necklaces, lips, ears, and forehead. A crest has broken off from the crown.

51 FACE WITH CAT'S WHISKER MARKS
12th/15th century
Terracotta; h. 12.5 cm. (5 in.)
From the Grove of Olokun Walode, Ife
National Museum, Lagos, S91.L9

One of the most delicately modeled Ife
pieces, this fragment was part of a larger
terracotta sculpture. The cat's whisker
marks occur on several Ife sculptures but
are nowadays characteristic of the Nupe,
who live to the north of the Yoruba. There
have been considerable changes in tribal
markings, however, since the Classical
period of Ife art, and it has been said that
the southern Nupe took this mark from the
Yoruba. This is one of a number of fragments found in the course of building and
farming which were brought together and
placed in the Olokun Grove of the Walode
family (*opposite*).

52 HEAD FROM A FIGURE
12th/15th century
Terracotta; h. 12.8 cm. (5 in.)
From Otutu Compound, Ife
Museum of Ife Antiquities, 23.61

This terracotta head — like many Ife sculptures — was found eroding from the ground
surface. It is very delicately modeled, with
small facial features. The way in which the
hair is represented is so far unparalleled on
other Ife works. All the Ife sculptures in
bronze and terracotta were probably originally painted.

53 HEAD FROM A FIGURE

12th/15th century
Terracotta; h. 16 cm. (6¼ in.)
From Ife
National Museum, Lagos, 79.R.6 (Ife 305)

Like many of the Ife terracotta heads, this piece has a hole in its beadwork
cap into which a crest, or perhaps an egret feather, was originally fitted.
It is in unusually fresh condition (*opposite*).

54 HEAD WITH FLARED HAIRDRESS

12th/15th century
Terracotta; h. 18 cm. (7 in.)
From Aba Ayinkinni, Oshi-Shoko (16 miles
south of Ife)
National Museum, Lagos (Ife 67.28a)

This head from a figure has the hair
dressed into a flaring shape on top, a
common hairstyle in the Ife sculptures but
represented here in an exaggerated form.
The sculpture is thickly encrusted with red
paint. A number of typical Ife sculptures
have been found well outside the city itself.

Another of the potlids found at Lafogido, this mythical animal might possibly be a hippopotamus. The all-over decoration of the head includes a herringbone pattern, incised diamond shapes, and a royal crest prominently displayed in the middle of the forehead. On the top of the head are either feathers or possibly *akoko* leaves (nos. 70 and 71), which present-day Yoruba use when installing a new chief or king (*opposite*).

This elephant's head is one of several potlids found at a site that may well be a royal tomb (fig. 7). The restraint Ife artists exhibited in the decoration and depiction of the human form seems to have loosened when the subject was an animal. The elephant's head is elaborately decorated with herring-bone pattern and crested headdress, indicating its royal status, and sits on a flat base ornamented with beads and feathers with its trunk curved to one side.

57 CYLINDRICAL REPRESENTATION OF A HUMAN HEAD

12th/15th century
Terracotta; h. 16 cm. (6⅜ in.)
From Abiri, near Ife
Museum of Ife Antiquities, AB 121

Ife heads are not invariably naturalistic. This is one of a group of highly abstract representations of the human head found alongside very naturalistic ones, suggesting that the two styles were contemporaneous. Compare also figure 20, which proved that this was in fact the case.

58 SPHERICAL RITUAL POT

12th/15th century
Terracotta; h. 24.9 cm. (9¹³⁄₁₆ in.)
From Koiwo Layout, Ife
National Museum, Lagos, 79.R.13

This spherical pot with relief decorations features a head with snakes issuing from its nostrils, a motif seen also in Owo, Benin, and Tsoede works (nos. 73 and 93). The other motifs are, in order, a pair of ceremonial staffs (*edan*), a nude woman, a different ceremonial staff, traces of a missing motif, a pair of bushcow (buffalo) horns (no. 59), a drum, a metal bracelet, a shrine with what may be human skulls at the base (judging from another similar pot), and a decapitated head and two snakes above, a bundle of sticks (?), a machete, and a calabash (*opposite*).

59 FEMALE FIGURE HOLDING TWO BUSHCOW HORNS

12th/15th century
Terracotta; h. 24.9 cm. (9¹³/₁₆ in.)
From a gravel-pit, believed to be on
Obalara's Land, Ife
National Museum, Lagos, 71.1.534

There are a number of small figures from Ife that appear to have
been parts of tableaux or group-
ings on a single support. This
piece with its head turned to the
side and its flat unfinished back
may have been part of one. The
figure wears a long wrapper and
carries a pair of bushcow (buffalo) horns in her hands (nos. 58
and 72, and compare nos. 44 and
45). Bushcow horns are nowadays associated with the cult of
Oya, goddess of the powerful
wind which precedes the thun-
derstorm, and goddess of the
River Niger. Her temperament
is thought to resemble that of a
bushcow.

OWO

60 HEAD FROM A FIGURE

c. 15th century
Terracotta; h. 17.4 cm. (6⅞ in.)
From Igbo'Laja, Owo
National Museum, Lagos, 73.2.7

Owo is a Yoruba city-state roughly halfway between Ife and Benin, and its art shows links to both cultures. This cool, serene head in the Ife art tradition was probably executed in Owo. The work exhibits such Ife characteristics as parallel striation marks on the face, the overlap of the corners of the lower lid by the upper one, the groove parallel to the edge of the upper lid, the impressed corners of the mouth, and the raised edge of the lips. The eyebrow ridges are more prominent than is usual on Ife terracottas.

61 HEAD

c. 15th century
Terracotta; h. 15 cm. (5^{15}/$_{16}$ in.)
From Igbo'Laja, Owo
National Museum, Lagos, 79.R.15

Although this piece is greatly abraded, Ife
facial characteristics are clearly evident.
The accurate portrayal of the face bones
can still be seen, which makes the head
unique among terracotta sculptures from
both Ife and Owo. It was recovered from
the priest in charge of the site, who had
pierced it to wear as a ceremonial pendant
(fig. 11).

116

62 HAND HOLDING A HEAD

c. 15th century
Terracotta; h. 7.6 cm. (3 in.)
From Igbo'Laja, Owo
National Museum, Lagos, 73.2.6

The flat face with eyes that echo the shape
of the mouth makes this head an abstract
work of great beauty and mystery. Behind
its left ear are the fingers of a hand that
holds it. This suggests that the head has
been decapitated, in which case this would
be further evidence of the theme of sacrifice that dominates this site (nos. 66–69).

63 BEARDED HEAD FROM A FIGURE

c. 15th century
Terracotta; h. 11 cm. (4⅝₆ in.)
From Igbo'Laja, Owo
National Museum, Lagos, 73.2.3

This frowning man — with his deeply furrowed brow, pronounced eye-
balls, flared nostrils, and strong mouth — is a highly individual and
expressive portrait. The way in which the cap is worn also differs from
usual. The beard, sideburn, and ear on his right side are carefully
depicted, while on the left the beard is missing and the ear is crudely
modeled. This suggests that it was not freestanding but part of a larger
sculpture, perhaps in the form of a tableau (*opposite*).

64 HEAD WITH PART OF TORSO

c. 15th century
Terracotta; h. 9.2 cm. (3⅝ in.)
From Igbo'Laja, Owo
National Museum, Lagos, 73.2.2

Exhibiting striations and eyes in
the style of Ife art, this small figure, with its upturned head and
slightly hunched back, engages
the viewer through its intense
gaze. It shows a sense of move-
ment unlike other figures, which
are rather static. Again, the broken surface on the left side of the
face indicates that it was attached
to another object or was a figure
from a tableau.

119

65 UPPER HALF OF A FIGURE

c. 15th century
Terracotta; h. 25 cm. (9¹³/₁₆ in.)
From Igbo'Laja, Owo
National Museum, Lagos, 73.2.1

The careful modeling of the head contrasting with the coarser treatment
of the body is typical of the sculptures found at Owo. This figure wears
an unusual necklace of beads and tassels, and a string of beads at the
waist where the costume covering the lower part of the body begins. The
position of the beaded forearms and the expressive mouth give the figure an uncommon vitality, though the head sits awkwardly on the trunk
(*opposite*).

66 WOMAN HOLDING A COCK

c. 15th century
Terracotta; h. 20.1 cm. (7¹⁵/₁₆ in.)
From Igbo'Laja, Owo
National Museum, Lagos, 73.2.22

The theme of sacrifice runs through much
of the art from Igbo'Laja. Here, a woman
holding a cock under her arm stands ready
to make her offering. The squat proportions
of this figure are characteristic of Owo
sculpture. The wrapper is folded down at
the top and is held to the body by a sash
tied around the waist.

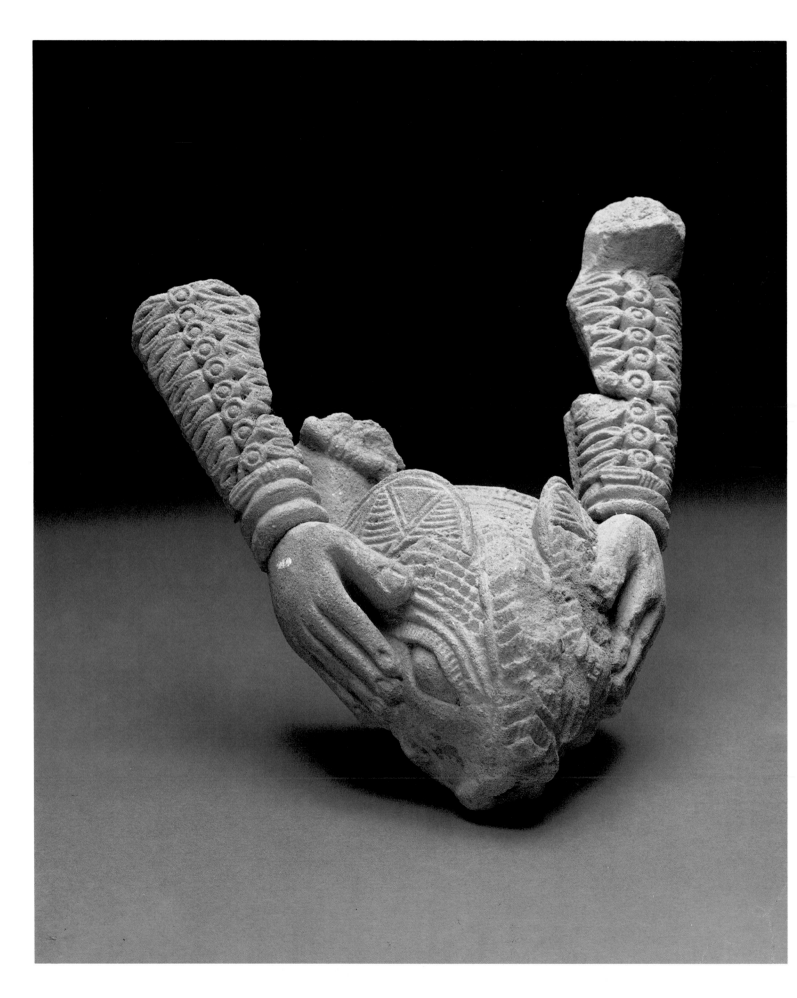

67 ARMS HOLDING AN ANIMAL'S HEAD

c. 15th century
Terracotta; h. 36 cm. (14 3/16 in.)
From Igbo'Laja, Owo
National Museum, Lagos, 73.2.62

It is not possible to identify with certainty the animal being presented here for sacrifice by a pair of heavily beaded forearms, although it is possibly a ram or an elephant. While the all-over ornamentation of the animal is reminiscent of Ife works (nos. 55 and 56), this animal is much more highly stylized, particularly in the disc-shaped ears decorated with incised triangles. The person making the presentation might have been royal, judging by the heavily clad arms, though none of the heads from the site wears a crown (*opposite*).

68 HAND HOLDING A SMALL ANIMAL

c. 15th century
Terracotta; h. 16 cm. (6 5/16 in.)
From Igbo'Laja, Owo
National Museum, Lagos, 73.2.43

Another work illustrating the importance of sacrifice in the sculptures from Igbo'Laja is this hand, presenting a lizard or rat in its palm. Note the ring around the thumb, the heavily beaded forearm, and the characteristic triangular nails.

69 COCK

c. 15th century
Terracotta; h. 11 cm. (4⁵/16 in.)
From Igbo'Laja, Owo
National Museum, Lagos, 72.2.63

A naturalistic representation of a cock with well-defined comb, beak,
cockles, and feathers, this work, with its cross-hatched patterning and
pupil-less eyes, recalls Ife interpretations of an elephant and a mythical
animal (nos. 55 and 56).

70 HAND HOLDING A BUNCH OF *AKOKO* LEAVES

c. 15th century
Terracotta; h. 10 cm. (3¹⁵⁄₁₆ in.)
From Igbo'Laja, Owo
National Museum, Lagos, 79.R.16

Certain trees and their leaves and branches are sacred in Yoruba culture. For example, *peregun* trees (*Dracaena fragrans*) are usually planted around sacred places to indicate their nature publicly, while leaves from the *akoko* tree are used especially in installation ceremonies of chiefs and kings. *Akoko* trees are also planted in sacred places; the foot of such trees often becomes an open shrine where sacrifices and prayers are offered. Here, a leafy branch covers most of the hand that holds it, although the thumb with its distinctive triangular nail is clearly visible.

71 HAND HOLDING AN *AKOKO* LEAF

c. 15th century
Terracotta; h. 11 cm. (4⁵⁄₁₆ in.)
From Igbo'Laja, Owo
National Museum, Lagos, 73.2.47

This hand holds an *akoko* leaf — a tree still regarded as sacred in the Yoruba culture. When the King is installed, he is given *akoko* leaves to indicate the authority with which he is being invested. It is also to wish the King long life, since these trees are remarkable for their longevity.

72 HAND HOLDING CROSSED HORNS

c. 15th century
Terracotta; l. 11.2 cm. (4⁷⁄₁₆ in.)
From Igbo'Laja, Owo
National Museum, Lagos, 73.2.46

This fragment of a figure represents a pair of horns, possibly of a bushcow or antelope, held in separate hands, only one of which has survived. Horns are often used as containers for magical substances, either singly (nos. 44 and 45) or in pairs (nos. 58 and 59), and this may be what is represented here.

73 FRAGMENT FROM A RITUAL POT WITH A FACE

c. 15th century
Terracotta; h. 10.8 cm. (4¼ in.)
From Igbo'Laja, Owo
National Museum, Lagos, 73.2.71

The precise significance of this motif, a face with snakes issuing from the nostrils, is lost in antiquity, though we may suppose that the snakes relate to the breath, which is identified with the soul in many parts of the world. This form of the motif, with horns over the forehead, occurs also in Ife and Benin works, and on the Tsoede bronzes (no. 93) and suggests that all these traditions are drawing the motif from a common source.

74 FRAGMENT WITH A MUDFISH SWALLOWING A PRAWN OR LOBSTER

c. 15th century
Terracotta; 1. 13 cm. (5⅛ in.)
From Igbo'Laja, Owo
National Museum, Lagos, 73.2.83

This fragment, probably broken off a pot, depicts a mudfish (catfish) with the hind portion of a prawn or a lobster in its mouth. The mudfish is a motif quite often found in Benin art (no. 88).

75 FRAGMENT OF A HEAD

c. 15th century
Terracotta; h. 6.8 cm. (2¹¹/₁₆ in.)
From Igbo'Laja, Owo
National Museum, Lagos, 73.2.14

This small fragment is a piece of great importance because of the four short marks above the eyes, which are unmistakably Benin scarification marks (nos. 76–78) and prove the connection between these two cultures. Two such face fragments were recovered from the excavation.

BENIN

76 QUEEN MOTHER HEAD
Early 16th century (Early Period)
Bronze; h. 51 cm. (20 in.)
From Benin
National Museum, Lagos, 79.R.17

Benin, the capital city of the Edo-speaking people, lies about seventy miles south of Owo and one hundred twenty miles southeast of Ife. This magnificent Queen Mother is one of the most famous bronze heads from Benin. It is said that Oba Esigie (ruled up to c. 1550) was the first to confer the title of Queen Mother on his mother, Idia, and that ever since each Oba, or King, has conferred the title on his mother three years after his accession. It was during Esigie's reign that trade with the Portuguese first made metal freely available, and this seems to have stimulated the artists to invent new artistic forms.

78 HEAD

Late 15th/mid-16th century (Early/Middle Period)
Terracotta; h. 21 cm. (8¼ in.)
From Benin
National Museum, Lagos, 60.3.2

The bronzesmiths had their own quarters in Benin City, where an altar was set up to Igueghae, the man from Ife who is said to have introduced bronze casting to Benin. Upon the altar were several terracotta heads like this one, which clearly follows the form of number 77, sculptures with the collar close to the neck and the hair represented rather than the crown as on later heads (*opposite*).

77 MEMORIAL HEAD

15th/early 16th century (Early Period)
Bronze; h. 21 cm. (8¼ in.)
From Benin
National Museum, Lagos, 54.15.7

According to oral tradition, bronze casting was introduced into Benin from Ife toward the end of the fourteenth century, but clearly an art tradition was already established there, as can be seen in the distinctively Benin style of this early memorial head of an Oba. Bronze memorial heads were made throughout Benin history, but the earliest ones, of which this is a fine example, are the most naturalistic and beautiful. All bronze casting and ivory carving were in the service of the Oba, making Benin art a royal one in the true sense.

130

79 HEAD IN UDO STYLE

16th/17th century (Middle Period)
Bronze; h. 23.5 cm. (9 1/4 in.)
From Benin
National Museum, Lagos, 56.2.7

This bronze head is cast in a style connected with a village called Udo, located
about forty miles from Benin. Udo
attempted to rival Benin City and this
piece, one of thirteen similar ones, represents the Udo version of the Early Period
memorial heads like number 77, though
two examples have given thermoluminescence dates around the end of the sixteenth
century, that is, in the Middle Period. The
Udo works, while clearly provincial in
style, show a vitality that is lacking in the
works they copy. They also have a rectangular slot in the back that is not found in
Benin pieces (*opposite*).

80 STANDING FIGURE OF A MESSENGER

Mid- to late 16th century (Early/Middle Period)
Bronze; h. 63.5 cm. (25 in.)
From Benin
National Museum, Lagos, 54.15.8

This fine bronze figure represents the royal
messenger who carried the emblems of authority from Ife to Benin when a new King
was installed. These emblems, the Portuguese sources record, were a bronze cap, a
cross, and a staff. After performing this
service, he was given a cross to wear and
became a free man. Since this figure is
apparently wearing the royal insignia, it
might be thought that he represents the
new King, but the cat's whisker scarification (no. 51) points to his being a foreigner
and thus probably a slave.

81-82 PAIR OF LEOPARDS
Mid-16th century (Early/Middle Period)
Bronze; 1. 69 cm. (27³/16 in.)
From Benin
National Museum, Lagos, 52.13.1, 52.13.2

Bronze leopards like this magnificent pair were placed on royal ancestor altars. These are aquamanile — water vessels filled through the top of the head, from which water could be poured through the nostrils during ceremonies. The Oba actually kept live leopards at court and employed a special keeper to look after them. The Benin artists were obviously familiar with their subject. Their sculptures combine an interest in well-observed detail, like the menacing jaws, spotted fur, alert ears, and piercing eyes, with a fine sense of overall design.

83 PLAQUE SHOWING TWO MUSICIANS
Late 16th/early 17th century (Middle Period)
Bronze; h. 48.5 cm. (19¹/8 in.)
From Benin
National Museum, Lagos, 50.30.8

Benin art spans about five centuries and comprises some thousands of
pieces. Art historians have attempted to date these stylistically, working
in both directions from the Middle Period, which is defined as the time
during which the plaques were made. This is thought to cover the later
part of the sixteenth and most of the seventeenth century. It has been
suggested that the rectangular form of the plaques, which rarely occurs
in African art except in sculpted doors, is based on the pictures the Bini
saw in European books. This example depicts two musicians, one striking
an ivory bell and the other shaking a rattle (*opposite*).

84 PLAQUE SHOWING TWO MEN
SWINGING ON ROPES
16th century (Middle Period)
Bronze; h. 43 cm. (16¹⁵/16 in.)
From Benin
National Museum, Lagos, 48.36.40

The plaques were used to decorate the
wooden columns that supported the roof of
the Oba's Palace, and the holes through
which they were nailed are clearly evident.
Many plaques show scenes of court life.
This plaque depicts part of a festival, no
longer performed, called *Isiokuo*, which
was a war ritual in honor of the god Ogun.
The ritual included an acrobatic dance,
called *Amufi*, represented on this plaque,
which recalls a legendary war against the
sky. Three ibises, birds of disaster, are
perched in the branches of the tree.

137

17th century (Middle Period)
Bronze; h. 53.5 cm. (21 in.)
From Benin
National Museum, Lagos, 48.36.1

This plaque shows the virtuoso skill with which the smiths of Benin handled relief in the later Middle Period. A warrior chief is shown in full ceremonial dress, a sword in his right hand and a spear in his left. He wears a cap decorated with feathers, a leopard's-tooth necklace, and a bell on his chest, while his two major attendants carry typical Benin shields. The small figures between are a swordkeeper and a trumpeter. The plaques were made during a time of increased contact with the Portuguese, which explains the inclusion of the head of the Portuguese at the upper left (*opposite*).

85 PLAQUE SHOWING THREE COURT ATTENDANTS

Late 16th/early 17th century (Middle Period)
Bronze; h. 49 cm. (19 1/4 in.)
From Benin
National Museum, Lagos, 50.30.6

In the lower left-hand corner of this plaque is a British Museum accession number, a reminder that the British removed most of Benin's art in the Punitive Expedition of 1897. Since World War II, the Nigerian government has made a great effort to recover Benin art and now holds the third largest collection of this material in the world. The quatrefoil motif on a stippled ground is a constant feature in the background of these plaques.

138

87 PLAQUE SHOWING CROCODILE

Late 16th/early 17th century (Middle Period)
Bronze; h. 19 cm.; w. 39.5 cm.
(h. 7½ in.; w. 15⁹/16 in.)
From Benin
National Museum, Lagos, 51.18.11

This crocodile is interpreted in a bird's-
eye view with large eyes, scaly texture,
wide belly, and anthropomorphic hands
and feet. The crocodile is believed by
many Bini to be the best sacrificial victim
to Olokun, god of the sea and wealth. It is
for them a symbol of power. Other animals
often represented in Benin art include
leopards, fishes, and snakes.

88 STOOL WITH SEAT IN FORM OF
INTERTWINED MUDFISH

16th century (Middle Period)
Bronze; h. 34 cm. (13³/₈ in.)
From Benin
National Museum, Lagos, 53.22.11

The mudfish is a royal Benin symbol and appears frequently in Benin
art. This elegantly stylized bronze stool features a top made of two intertwined mudfish joined to a circular base by a column. Their flattened
shape and the patterning of their barbels and scales create a wonderful
sense of how they move in water.

89 VESSEL

Perhaps 17th century (Middle Period)
Bronze; h. 22.5 cm. (8⁷/8 in.)
From Benin
National Museum, Lagos, 54.15.15

The handles of this vessel represent snakes with human beings in their mouths. A snail, tortoise, and drummer are also sculpted in relief on both sides. It originally had a hinged lid (*opposite*).

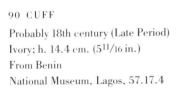

90 CUFF

Probably 18th century (Late Period)
Ivory; h. 14.4 cm. (5¹¹/16 in.)
From Benin
National Museum, Lagos, 57.17.4

One of the royal prerogatives in Benin was the right to half the ivory from the elephants killed by all hunters. One of each pair of tusks received the King's mark and many of these he then passed to his ivory carvers, some of whom came from Owo, like the artist who made this cuff. A tour de force of carving, the works consist of two pieces carved from a single block of ivory, the inner cylinder moving independently of the outer one. Thus the inner core, pierced with holes between motifs, acts as a kind of stippled background texture for the complex pattern of carvings on the outer part. Note once again the mudfish — a common motif in Benin art.

143

91 LIDDED BOWL

Possibly 16th century (Middle Period)
Ivory and brass; h. 22.5 cm. (8⁷/₈ in.)
From Benin
National Museum, Lagos, 53.22.10

This unusual bowl, constructed of several separate pieces of ivory, was found in the King of Benin's bedchamber. It is unusual in being decorated with strips of brass. The human faces and the interlace motifs are typical Benin designs.

THE TSOEDE
BRONZES

c. late 13th/14th century
Copper; h. 53.7 cm. (21⅛ in.)
From Tada
National Museum, Lagos, 79.R.18

This extraordinary casting, probably the most naturalistic sculpture
produced in Africa, was found in the remote Nupe village of Tada on the
right bank of the River Niger. It is a remarkably complex piece to have
been cast in copper. Although it is clearly in the Ife style (compare
especially nos. 39—41 and 44), it differs from all known Ife works in the
natural proportions of the head and limbs. The people of Tada used to take
it to the River Niger every Friday (they are Muslims nowadays) and scrub
it with gravel from the riverbed to ensure the fertility of themselves and
the fish on which they live. This washing is what produced the abraded
surface. While its unfortunate condition makes it appear almost
trancelike, one can sense the inner serenity and composure of the figure,
which is so characteristic of all other Ife works. It has been dated by
thermoluminescence to the late thirteenth or fourteenth century.

93 FIGURE OF A WARRIOR

c. early 14th/early 15th century
Tin bronze; h. 115 cm. (45¼ in.)
From Tada
National Museum, Lagos, 79.R.20

This large figure, one of the Tsoede
bronzes (nos. 92–96), wears an outer garment covered with cowrie shells, a necklace of leopard's teeth, and a pectoral
medallion with representations of a ram
and birds. His complex headdress features
a disc depicting a horned face with snakes
issuing from the nostrils. This motif, found
on Ife, Owo, and Benin works (nos. 58
and 73), has led scholars to suggest that
this work originated further south than
where it was found, possibly in Owo. It has
been dated by thermoluminescence to
between the early fourteenth and early fifteenth centuries.

94 FIGURE OF A BOWMAN

Probably c. early 14th/early 15th century
Tin bronze; h. 92 cm. (36¼ in.)
From Jebba Island
National Museum, Lagos, 79.R.19

This large statue of a bowman wearing body
armor, with a quiver of arrows on his back,
is one of nine bronzes found in the village
on Jebba Island and at Tada on the bank
of the River Niger. According to tradition,
they were transported there by a great
sixteenth-century hero, a slave named
Tsoede, who had escaped from Idah, the
Igala capital. While this work and the figure of a warrior (no. 93) exhibit some influence of Owo and Benin styles, they exhibit
unique characteristics, such as a kidney-
shaped mouth, bulging eyes with raised
outline, small head, tiny arms, and the
form of their costumes.

95 FIGURE WITH STAFF

Probably early 14th/16th century
Tin bronze; h. 42.5 cm. (16¾ in.)
From Tada
National Museum, Lagos, 79.R.21

This small standing figure carrying a staff
in his hand wears a decorated cap, necklace, and skirt. The kidney-shaped mouth
and large eyes with raised outline are seen
on several of the Tsoede bronzes (nos. 93
and 94). The disc-topped staff is found on
sculptures found in Benin but thought to
have been made in Owo (*opposite*).

150

96 STANDING FIGURE WITH HANDS CLASPED

Probably 16th or 17th century
Copper; h. 56.5 cm. (22¼ in.)
From Tada
National Museum, Lagos, 79.R.22

The large bulging eyes, protruding lips, and stylized ears of this figure are characteristics of late Ife art as it developed into the modern Yoruba style, from the sixteenth century onward (figs. 31 and 32 and no. 97). The gesture made by the hands, with one grasping the thumb of the other, is characteristic of the Ogboni Society, a secret society responsible for the cult of the earth in Yorubaland (no. 97).

OTHER WORKS

97 FIGURE OF ONILE

Probably 18th century
Brass; h. 106 cm. (41³/4 in.)
From Iperu
National Museum, Lagos, 65.4.53

This Yoruba work represents Onile, the spirit of the earth, who is the
center of the Ogboni cult. The very large eyes in the shape of half an
almond are characteristic of brass castings for the Ogboni Society. It is the
largest of four very similar castings.

98 SEATED FIGURE

Date undetermined (before 1850)
Soapstone; h. 67 cm. (26³/4 in.)
From Esie
National Museum, Esie, HT 260

The soapstone sculptures of Esie are an enigma. About eight hundred of them were found by the present inhabitants when they emigrated to the area either in the late eighteenth or early nineteenth century. As a way of explaining their origin, the local people tell stories of a group of visitors to the town having been turned to stone. Art historians and archaeologists have not done any better so far in explaining their origins (*opposite*).

99 SEATED FIGURE WITH SWORD

Date undetermined (before 1850)
Soapstone; h. 78 cm. (30¹¹/16 in.)
From Esie
National Museum, Esie, H348

The soapstone Esie figures mainly represent men and women sitting, and, rarely, kneeling; playing musical instruments; or holding machetes. The figures illustrated here share certain characteristics: both sit on stools with their hands on their knees, wear a triple-stranded necklace, and have similar elaborate hairdos.

100 FIGURE (*AKWANSHI*)

Date undetermined
(16th/19th century)
Stone; 114 cm. (44⅞ in.)
From Old Nkrigom, Cross River
National Museum, Lagos, 79.R.23

The earliest of the Ikom monoliths
from the Cross River area probably date back to the sixteenth
century, but they continued to be
made until the beginning of the
present century. More than three
hundred in number, they are
highly stylized but varied in
detail. The strange abstraction of
the style of these anthropomorphic relief sculptures makes them
seem even more mysterious than
the sculptures of Esie (nos. 98
and 99).

SELECTED BIBLIOGRAPHY

Works listed in this bibliography have been chosen with both the general reader and the scholar in mind. Those listings regarded as essential for the study of the art of ancient Nigeria are indicated by an asterisk. In the listings under the individual cultures, except for Nok, the work with an asterisk also contains a more complete bibliography on the culture. In the case of Ife, the bibliography from the basic work, which was published in 1967, has been brought up to date.

AFRICAN ART

Delange, Jacqueline. 1974. *The Art and Peoples of Black Africa*. New York: E. P. Dutton.

Gaskin, L. J. P. 1965. *A Bibliography of African Art*. London: International African Institute.

Leiris, Michel, and Delange, Jacqueline. 1968. *African Art*. New York: Golden Press.

Leuzinger, Elsy. 1977. *The Art of Black Africa*. New York: Rizzoli.

Western, Dominique Coulet. 1975. *A Bibliography of the Arts of Africa*. Waltham, Mass.: African Studies Association.

Willett, Frank. 1971. *African Art: An Introduction*. London: Thames and Hudson, and New York: Frederick Praeger.

NIGERIAN ART

*Eyo, Ekpo, 1977. *Two Thousand Years Nigerian Art*. Lagos: Federal Department of Antiquities.

Fagg, William. 1963. *Nigerian Images*. London: Lund Humphries.

Forman, Werner, and Brentjes, Burchard. 1967. *Alte Afrikanische Plastik*. Leipzig: Koehler and Amelang.

Ita, Nduntuei O. 1971. *A Bibliography of Nigeria*. London: Cass.

*Shaw, Thurstan. 1978. *Nigeria: Its Archaeology and Early History*. London: Thames and Hudson.

Shaw, Thurstan, and Vandenburg, Joel. 1969. *A Bibliography of Nigerian Archaeology*. Ibadan: Ibadan University Press.

NOK

Fagg, Angela. 1972. "A Preliminary Report on an Occupation Site in the Nok Valley, Nigeria," *West African Journal of Archaeology* 2: 75–9.

Fagg, Bernard E. B. 1945. "A Preliminary Note on a New Series of Pottery Figures from Northern Nigeria," *Africa* 15 (1): 21–2.

———. 1946. "Archaeological Notes from Northern Nigeria," *Man* 46: no.48, pp. 49–55.

———. 1956. "A Life-size Terracotta Head from Nok," *Man* 56: no. 95, p. 89.

———. 1956. "The Nok Culture," *West African Review* 156 (December): 1083–7.

————. 1959. "The Nok Culture in Prehistory," *Journal of the Historical Society of Nigeria* 1 (4): 288–93.

————. 1962. "The Nok Terracottas in West African Art History," *Actes du IVe Congrès Panafricain de Préhistoire*, Tervuren. Sect. 3: 445–50.

————. 1969. "Recent Work in West Africa: New Light on the Nok Culture," *World Archaeology* 1 (1): 41–50.

*————. 1977. *Nok Terracottas*. Lagos: The Nigerian Museum, and London: Ethnographica.

Willett, Frank. 1967. *Ife in the History of West African Sculpture*. London: Thames and Hudson, and New York: McGraw-Hill Book Company.

YELWA

Breternitz, David A. 1975. "Rescue Archaeology in the Kainji Reservoir Area 1968," *West African Journal of Archaeology* 5: 91–151.

Hartle, Donald D. 1970. "Preliminary Report of the University of Ibadan's Kainji Rescue Archaeology Project, 1968," *West African Archaeological Newsletter* 12: 7–19.

*Priddy, A. J. 1970. "RS/63/32: An Iron Age Site near Yelwa, Sokoto Province: Preliminary Report," *West African Archaeological Newsletter* 12: 20–32.

IGBO-UKWU

Davison, Claire C. 1972. *Glass Beads in African Archaeology: Results of Neutron Activation Analysis, Supplemented by Results of X-Ray Fluorescence Analysis*. Berkeley, Cal.: Lawrence Berkeley Laboratory LBL–1240.

Field, J. O. 1940. "Bronze Castings found at Igbo, Southern Nigeria," *Man* 40: no. 1, pp. 1–6.

Jones, G. I. 1939. "Ibo Bronzes from the Awka Division," *Nigerian Field* 8 (4): 164–7.

Lawal, Babatunde. 1972. "Archaeological Excavations at Igbo-Ukwu — A Reassessment," *Odu*, n.s. 8: 72–97.

————. 1972. "The Igbo-Ukwu Bronzes: A Search for the Economic Evidence," *Journal of the Historical Society of Nigeria* 6 (3): 1–8.

————. 1973. "Dating Problems at Igbo-Ukwu," *Journal of African History* 14 (1): 1–8.

*Shaw, Thurstan. 1970. *Igbo-Ukwu: An Account of Archaeological Discoveries in eastern Nigeria*. 2 vols. London: Faber and Faber, and Evanston: Northwestern University Press.

————. 1970. "The Analysis of West African Bronzes: A Summary of the Evidence," *Ibadan* 28: 80–9.

————. 1975. "Those Igbo-Ukwu Radiocarbon Dates: Facts, Fictions and Probabilities," *Journal of African History* 16 (4): 503–17.

————. 1977. *Unearthing Igbo-Ukwu*. London: Oxford University Press, and Ibadan: Ibadan University Press.

IFE

Anonymous. 1948. "Donatellos of Medieval Africa: The Ife Bronze Portrait Heads," *Illustrated London News*, 213, July 3: 24.

Davison, Claire C. 1972. *Glass Beads in African Archaeology: Results of Neutron Activation Analysis, Supplemented by Results of X-Ray Fluorescence Analysis*, Berkeley, Cal.: Lawrence Berkeley Laboratory LBL–1240.

Eluyemi, Omotoso. 1975. "New Terracotta Finds at Oke-Eso Ife," *African Arts* 9 (1): 32–5.

————. 1976. "Egbejoda Excavations, Nigeria, 1970," *West African Journal of Archaeology* 6: 101–8.

————. 1977. "Terracotta Sculpture from Obalara's Compound, Ile-Ife," *African Arts* 10 (3): 41.

Eyo, Ekpo. 1970. "1969 Excavations Ile-Ife," *African Arts* 3 (2): 44.

————. 1974. "Odo Ogbe Street and Lafogido; Contrasting Archaeological Sites in Ile-Ife, Western Nigeria," *West African Journal of Archaeology* 4: 99–109.

————. 1974. *Recent Excavations at Ife and Owo and Their Implications for Ife, Owo and Benin Studies*. Unpublished Ph.D. thesis, University of Ibadan.

Frobenius, Leo. 1913. *The Voice of Africa*. 2 vols. London: Hutchinson and Co. (Reprinted 1968, New York and London: Benjamin Blom.)

————. 1949. *Mythologie de l'Atlantide*. Paris: Payot.

Garlake, Peter. 1974. "Excavations at Obalara's Land: An Interim Report," *West African Journal of Archaeology* 4: 111–48.

————. "Excavations on the Woye Asiri Land in Ife, Western Nigeria," *West African Journal of Archaeology* 7. (Forthcoming.)

Werner, O., and Willett, Frank. 1975. "The Composition of Brasses from Ife and Benin," *Archaeometry* 17 (2): 141–63.

*Willett, Frank. 1967. *Ife in the History of West African Sculpture*. London: Thames and Hudson, and New York: McGraw-Hill Book Company.

————. 1967. "Ife in Nigerian Art," *African Arts* 1 (1): 30–5.

———. 1975. "Radiocarbon Dates and Cire-perdue Casting in Ife and Benin," *Abh. u. Ber. des Staatlichen Museum für Völkerkunde Dresden* 34: 291–300.

———. 1977. *Baubles, Bangles and Beads: Trade Contacts of Medieval Ife*. Edinburgh: Centre of African Studies.

——— and Fleming, S. J. 1976. "A Catalogue of Important Nigerian Copper-Alloy Castings Dated by Thermoluminescence," *Archaeometry* 18 (2): 135–46.

OWO

Akintoye, S. A. 1969. "The North-Eastern Districts of the Yoruba Country and the Benin Kingdom," *Journal of the Historical Society of Nigeria* 4(4): 539–53.

Ashara, Chief M. B. 1966. *The History of Owo*, 2nd edition. Unpublished.

Egharevba, Jacob. 1960, 1968. *A Short History of Benin*. Ibadan: Ibadan University Press.

Eyo, Ekpo. 1972. "New Treasures from Nigeria," *Expedition* 14 (2).

*———. 1974. *Recent Excavations at Ife and Owo and Their Implications for Ife, Owo and Benin Studies*. Unpublished Ph.D. thesis, University of Ibadan.

———. 1976. "Igbo'Laja, Owo," *West African Journal of Archaeology* 6: 37–58.

Fagg, W. B. 1951. "Tribal Sculpture and the Festival of Britain," *Man* 51: no. 124, pp. 73–6.

Fraser, Douglas. 1975. "Tsoede Bronzes and Owo Art," *African Arts* 8 (3): 30–5.

Willett, Frank. 1973. "The Benin Museum Collection," *African Arts* 6(4): 8–17, 94.

BENIN

Ben-Amos, Paula. 1968. *Bibliography of Benin Art*. Primitive Art Bibliographies, no. VI. New York: The Museum of Primitive Art.

———. 1973. "Symbolism in Olokun Mud Art," *African Arts* 6 (4): 28–31, 95.

———. 1976. "Men and Animals in Benin Art," *Man* (n.s.) 11: 243–52.

Connah, Graham. 1975. *The Archaeology of Benin: Excavations and other researches in and around Benin City, Nigeria*. Oxford: Clarendon Press.

*Dark, Philip J. C. 1973. *An Introduction to Benin Art and Technology*. Oxford: Clarendon Press.

———. 1973. "Brass Casting in West Africa," *African Arts* 6 (4): 50–3, 94.

———. 1975. "Benin Bronze Heads: Styles and Chronology," in *African Images: Essays in African Iconology*, edited by Daniel F. McCall and Edna G. Bay. New York, London: Africana Publishing Co.

———. *Summary Catalogue of Benin Art*. (Forthcoming.)

——— with Forman, W. and B. 1960. *Benin Art*. London: Batchworth Press.

Egharevba, Jacob. 1960, 1968. *A Short History of Benin*. Ibadan: Ibadan University Press.

Fagg, William. 1970. *Divine Kingship in Africa*. London: British Museum.

Luschan, Felix von. 1919. *Die Altertümer von Benin*. 3 vols. Berlin and Leipzig: Vereinigung Wissenschaftlicher Verleger. (Reprinted 1968. New York: Hacker Art Books.)

Pitt-Rivers, L. F. 1900. *Antique Works of Art from Benin*. London: Harrison Printers. (Reprinted 1968. New York: Hacker Art Books.)

Read, C. H., and Dalton, O. M. 1899. *Antiquities from the City of Benin and Other Parts of West Africa in the British Museum*. London: British Museum. (Reprinted 1973. New York: Hacker Art Books.)

Roth, H. Ling. 1903. *Great Benin: Its Customs, Art and Horrors*. Halifax, England: A. King and Sons. (Reprinted 1968. London: Routledge and Kegan Paul.)

Shaw, Thurstan. 1969. "Further Spectrographic Analyses of Nigerian Bronzes," *Archaeometry* 11: 85–98.

Werner, O. 1970. "Metallurgische Untersuchungen der Benin — Bronzen des Museum für Völkerkunde Berlin," *Baessler Archiv*. 18: 71–153.

——— and Willett, F. 1975. "The Composition of Brasses from Ife and Benin," *Archaeometry* 17 (2): 141–56.

Willett, Frank. 1973. "The Benin Museum Collection," *African Arts* 6 (4): 8–17, 94.

———. 1975. "Radiocarbon Dates and Cire-perdue Casting at Ife and Benin," *Abh. u. Ber. des Staatlichen Museum für Völkerkunde Dresden* 34: 291–300.

——— and Fleming, S. J. 1976. "A Catalogue of Important Nigerian Copper-alloy Castings Dated by Thermoluminescence," *Archaeometry* 18 (2): 135–46.

TSOEDE

Eccles, P. 1962. "Nupe Bronzes," *Nigeria Magazine* 73: 13–25.

Fagg, William. 1960. "The Mysterious Bronzes of Jebba and Tada, Northern Nigeria," *Illustrated London News*, 236, no. 6290, Feb. 20: 297–9.

Fraser, Douglas. 1975. "Tsoede Bronzes and Owo Art," *African Arts* 8 (3): 30–5.

Shaw, Thurstan. 1969. "Further Spectrographic Analyses of Nigerian Bronzes," *Archaeometry* 11: 85–98.

Thompson, Robert Farris. 1970. "The Sign of the Divine King: An Essay on Yoruba Bead-embroidered Crowns with Veil and Bird Decorations," *African Arts* 3 (3): 8–17, 74–78, 80.

Willett, Frank. 1967. *Ife in the History of West African Sculpture*. London: Thames and Hudson, and New York: McGraw-Hill Book Company.

———. 1973. "The Benin Museum Collection," *African Arts* 6 (4): 8–17, 94.

——— and Fleming, S. J. 1976. "A Catalogue of Important Nigerian Copper-Alloy Castings Dated by Thermoluminescence," *Archaeometry* 18 (2): 135–46.

ESIE

Allison, Philip. 1968. *African Stone Sculpture*. London: Lund Humphries, and New York: Frederick Praeger.

*Stevens, Phillips, Jr. 1978. *The Stone Images of Esie, Nigeria*. Ibadan: Ibadan University Press, and Lagos: Federal Department of Antiquities.

IKOM

Allison, Philip. 1968. *African Stone Sculpture*. London: Lund Humphries, and New York: Frederick Praeger.

*———. 1968. *Cross River Monoliths*. Lagos: Federal Department of Antiquities.

YORUBA

*Thompson, Robert Farris. 1971. *Black Gods and Kings: Yoruba Art at UCLA*. Los Angeles: University of California, Museum and Laboratories of Ethnic Arts and Technology. (Reprinted 1976. Bloomington and London: Indiana University Press.)

Printed by A. Colish, Inc., Mount Vernon, New York
Bound by Economy Bookbinding Corporation, Kearny, New Jersey